WINDOWBOXES
and
HANGING BASKETS

WINDOWBOXES
and
HANGING BASKETS

CLAIRE PHOENIX

PHOTOGRAPHS BY SPIKE POWELL AND GLYN BARNEY

MEREHURST

For Em, Robert, Rupert and Holly

Published in 1995 by Merehurst Limited
Ferry House, 51–57 Lacy Road, Putney, London SW15 1PR, England

Reprinted 1995

Editor: Lesley Young
Designer: Maggie Aldred
Illustrator: Mike Shoebridge
Photographers: Spike Powell and Glyn Barney
Additional photographs p. 28 top right and p. 47 by Eric Crichton;
p. 12 bottom right by Stephen Crowdy; p. 25 top right and bottom left
by Clive Nichols.
Cover photographs: Spike Powell

Typeset by Goodfellow & Egan Ltd., Cambridge
Colour separation by Fotographics Ltd, UK–Hong Kong
Printed in Italy by Canale & C., S.p.A

CONTENTS

INTRODUCTION

The Smallest Garden

Creating your own hanging baskets and windowboxes is the simplest way to try out all sorts of gardening – from alpines to strawberries, spring bulbs to tomatoes. With the minimum outlay you can achieve very satisfying results.

Whether you have gardened for years or have no garden at all, a hanging basket or windowbox is the ideal starting point. This book contains lots of ideas to show you just how different various combinations of classic plants can look – it's part of their beauty that they never have quite the same appearance twice. More importantly, I also hope to tempt you to try some more unusual combinations.

There are lots of gardening tips, plus clear, step-by-step photographs and key illustrations so that you will know exactly what to plant where.

There are sections on the vital elements of soil, watering and plant care. Ideas are given for more unusual containers and for decorating containers with stencilling and liming.

Of course, you could limit your hanging

baskets and windowboxes to a few warm summer months and opt for the more obvious plants such as pelargoniums, busy lizzies and ivy, but there are so many other lovely and easily grown plants to discover. Whether you have a difficult, shady spot to fill, or would like to attempt a more unusual wildflower windowbox there are ideas here to tempt you.

There are also schemes for the autumn and winter, when, as gardens begin to die down, there is an even greater need for colour in our lives. At this time, Christmas baskets and trugs can be used inside or outside in a reasonably sheltered position.

This book caters for a wide range of gardening knowledge and experience, from ideas for youngsters attempting their first baskets to stunning schemes grown from seed and cuttings. One section is devoted to single species baskets, which can be particularly effective, and another to foliage planting which makes a refreshing contrast to brightly coloured beds and borders.

Enjoy browsing through the various schemes and do not be afraid of attempting something a little different – you are likely to be surprised and delighted with the results.

UNUSUAL WINDOWBOXES

From bicycle baskets to trugs, watering cans to brightly coloured plastic pots there are more ways to arrange plants than in a traditional windowbox.

From pottery to plastic, stone to wrought iron, there are more types of windowbox than you can imagine. A stroll around a nearby garden centre or along the streets of your home town can give you ideas of the containers you would – or perhaps would not – like to use. You may come across a wonderful old lead windowbox or an excellent plastic fake. Each type of windowbox has its advantages and drawbacks. Stone is beautiful but extremely heavy, plastic is lightweight but not so attractive and can age badly, cracking and yellowing. However, when planted, plastic can be indiscernible from, say, terracotta and costs far less. Terracotta looks good and, being heavier than plastic, is more stable. It is also porous, however, which means that the compost can dry out in hot weather, and it is not always frost-proof.

Consider the plants you are planning to use. You may need to adjust your plans so that box and plants complement each other. There's no need always to opt for a purpose-made box or basket. Be a little inventive and use an old hamper or assorted tins and you could create an individual plant holder that will be greatly admired.

● Make the most of old galvanised watering cans by filling them with plants and arranging them along a sill. You will need to drill holes for drainage. Choose trailing plants such as these trailing petunia, 'Surfinia', and verbena, although the taller clary stand up effectively.

● An old bicycle basket makes a good windowbox, enhanced by the mass of pelargoniums. Line it with slit plastic, compost and slow-release fertiliser. Choose a sunny spot for pelargoniums and water regularly in hot spells. Hang by the leather straps on screwed-in wire.

• A rustic log provides a harmonious container for year-round windowbox arrangements. Here, chrysanthemums, marguerites and the warm variegated foliage of a coleus provide late summer and early autumn colour.

• Fill an old trug with a mass of soft colour and sit it on a sill, inside or out. Here fuchsias, busy lizzies (*Impatiens walleriana*) petunias and flossflower (*Ageratum*) mingle delicately with silver-leaved *Helichrysum petiolatum*.
Tip: Use plastic liner to keep the wood from rotting.

• A simple line-up of coloured pots in nature's clashing colours provides a refreshing contrast to more organised arrangements. From left to right, heliotrope, rock rose, oxalis, busy lizzie, pelargonium, marguerites, marigolds and plectranthus collude to create a pleasingly childlike array.

• Plant up an old beer crate by lining it first with slit plastic and then add crocks and compost. This version had a slatted base but you may need to drill drainage holes. It is deep enough for a hydrangea, scabious, petunias and marigolds to bloom happily.

9

HANGING BASKETS WITH A DIFFERENCE

From old kettles to colanders, unusual baskets are tucked away in corners just waiting to be filled with flowers. Seek a change from the traditional wire basket.

The earliest type of hanging basket was made of simple wires strung together in a lattice pattern. Now there are a great many different types, from plastic bowls on chains, with a reservoir to aid watering, to ornate 'bird cages' which make an attractive feature even when the basket is empty.

The most popular option is a plastic-coated wire basket which does not rust, unlike the earlier versions, and has plenty of spaces for planting from below. There are plastic versions of this type with vertical fins which make inserting plants even easier. There are also purpose-made hanging balls which break in half and then clip together again, where, in the past, two standard baskets had to be wired to form a sphere.

Wicker baskets can look extremely effective but are best lined with plastic to prevent excessive leaching of water and compost. Unusual containers, such as colanders and kettles, make good hanging baskets and are worth looking out for.

● Original cast-iron cauldrons, such as this, have been widely copied as lightweight plastic versions. If you are lucky enough to have an original, make sure your fixings are secure as they are weighty. A blend of oxalis, pelargonium, petunia and fuchsia creates a pleasing container.

● Make the most of an unusual basket – this one is made of green wire and bamboo – by planting harmonising colours. The simple green and white theme of white *Dianthus* and variegated ivy is particularly striking and does not detract from the container.

● Purpose-made wall pots are available in glazed and unglazed pottery – they make good holiday souvenirs. This terracotta version has a moulding of grapes and looks just right filled with oxalis, verbena and petunias.

● A three-tier, wire vegetable holder may be out of vogue in the kitchen but makes an excellent hanging basket. Here three apricot portulaca, with their fat, waxy leaves, make an eyecatching trailing arrangement that thrives best in full sun. Using the same plant for each layer is effective.

● A metal colander makes a pretty and unusual hanging basket. With drainage holes ready made, you simply need to hang it, using strong wire or hook-on chains. Planted with trailing petunias and campanula to tone in with the blue and white colander, it makes a picturesque corner.

● Hunt out an old kettle or oversize teapot for a more unusual hanging basket. Trailing plants such as creeping jenny, petunia and verbena combine with more upright marigolds and blue felicia for a colourful arrangement that makes passersby smile.

● Windowboxes are cheering on balconies where they please the small-scale gardener and passersby alike. Hanging baskets can look particularly attractive when colour-balanced with boxes below. Here fuchsias, petunias, verbena and busy lizzies create a striking show.

● Dahlias at the doorstep, hanging balls of trailing pelargoniums (*P.* 'Mini Cascade') and cascading fuchsias combine with a myriad plants in the border to make this row of terraced cottages one of the prettiest exteriors seen – or rather hidden.

● A typical town house. Here grey brick and stonework have been lifted with bright windowboxes of red pelargoniums (*P. hortorum* 'Red Elite'). A basket of trailing begonias, fuchsias and pelargoniums links with a border of flossflower (*Ageratum*) and more pelargoniums.

● A simple, pale grey frontage has been given a lift with a mass of trailing pink pelargoniums. To ensure such a wonderful display, you need to begin early in the season giving the plants a good start in a greenhouse if possible. A large, deep windowbox to retain moisture will also help.

12

CREATING AN IMPRESSION

Against any building backdrop, whether brick, stone or render, windowboxes and hanging baskets are a celebration of the season.

Wherever you live, a hanging basket or windowbox will make a lasting first impression on visitors.

This is your opportunity to create a welcoming windowbox or basket that says how much you care about your home. Decorating need not stop at immaculate paintwork – baskets and windowboxes will soften the exterior of your home and give it an inviting and perfectly finished appearance. A carefully tended windowbox or basket will bring pleasure to you and passersby for a whole season and, with carefully chosen planting, can act as a link between your home and garden.

Before selecting any plants, consider the exterior of your home. Will your basket or windowbox be mounted against brick, stone or render? Do you wish the colours of your plants to contrast or blend in? Could you plan a scheme to tone in with the paintwork or other house features or do you intend the plants to stand out in a bold display of colour?

Take a look at your neighbours' gardens and houses. Do you wish to create a complete contrast or do you wish to plant boxes and hanging baskets to tone in with the 'look' of your street. Don't just think of spring and summer. Lovely baskets and boxes can be planted for year-round enjoyment.

● In a riot of colour, this bungalow has been given a vibrant facelift with balls of busy lizzie and marigold, baskets of pelargonium and lobelia and a contrasting border of *Ageratum* and marigold that is vivid enough to stop you in your tracks.

● This unusual cast-iron windowbox of pink trailing pelargoniums would be appreciated from both inside and out. On each side of the garage entrance baskets containing four varieties of fuchsia, pelargoniums and lobelia brighten what could be an otherwise dull area.

• Two brimming baskets and a stunning bank of summer flowers lift these garages out of the ordinary. Petunias, pendulous fuchsias and marigolds subtly enhance the pink of the rendered walls while softening the harder edges of the building.

• Glorious baskets of pelargoniums – both upright and trailing – petunias and lobelia. Prettily variegated Swedish ivy (*Nepeta*) and the light foliage of helichrysum echo the pale green of the door. When hanging baskets by a door, be aware of the final 'bulk' of the flowers in full bloom.

• Strong pink trailing verbena and pelargonium with stunning red busy lizzies and begonias are mixed with shades of lobelia (*Lobelia erinus* 'Rosamund' and *L. e.* 'Crystal Palace') to create a wonderful balance of colour against this blue door.

• A porch doorway is framed and softened with three baskets of pelargoniums, petunias, silvery helichrysum and lobelia. The colour scheme is followed through at ground level with wooden tubs filled with flowers in colours that complement the bright shades of the baskets.

MAKING AN ENTRANCE

Create a welcoming first impression with brimming baskets hanging by your door.

If the windows are the eyes of your home, then your doorway is its mouth and voice. The secret of these planting schemes is that they have all been carefully chosen to flatter the doorway and its surrounds. From a double garage to a disused cellar, all doorways benefit from complementary colour.

One of the joys of small-scale gardening is that, even when using similar plants, each basket and box is totally individual. The popular summer annuals – pelargoniums, petunias, fuchsias, busy lizzies and lobelia are each time arranged in differing proportions, using different varieties. Employing blue-and-pink-toned plants to echo a door colour makes an attractive arrangement that is easy on the eye.

Contrasting foliage plants add further interest, with the result that each basket is unique and can be planned to reflect the character of your home. Obviously, it is important to think ahead a little before fixing hanging baskets by a doorway. A basket that has just been planted takes up no more room than its own diameter. When in full bloom, however, the total area it occupies is considerably more. For this reason, do not set the baskets too close to the doorway, otherwise the petals and foliage will be damaged by people brushing past.

● An unused doorway looks inviting with this collection of pots and a bright hanging basket of marigolds, brachycome, verbena, lobelia and *Bidens aurea* beneath the arch of a leafy wisteria. Make sure that you do not allow foliage and plants to obscure a background feature too much.

● A light-coloured wooden door is given a fresh country feel when flanked by two colourful baskets. Lobelia, fuchsia, pelargonium and gold brachycome combine with the garden to create a welcoming entrance. Without the baskets, this doorway might look rather severe.

WINDOWS

Plant your windowbox to make the most of your window or to change its character completely.

Some windows will benefit more from hanging baskets and windowboxes than others. If your house is close to the road, has little or no front garden and many passersby, a basket or windowbox can have a noticeable effect and will be much admired.

Even if your windowbox is for your eyes alone, you will receive months of pleasure for relatively little outlay. It is worth planning the position of your hooks and boxes before you start. Take note of successful arrangements in your area and you will discover which sizes and combinations work best. You may find that windowboxes would work better above, rather than below, your window, provided they are easy to water.

One long windowbox is less likely to dry out than two smaller ones. You may wish to have a number of windowboxes or baskets arranged vertically rather than horizontally. Symmetrical baskets often work well, although it is rare to see such symmetry in nature! A number of small hanging baskets will need a great deal of care as these tend to dry out quickly; fewer, larger baskets may be a better choice and watering will prove less of a chore than with many small baskets.

Just as in art, everyone's taste in flowers differs. You may wish for single-colour planting, mixed colours or something completely different such as vegetables. Consider the next section, on season, size, soil and situation, before you make your final decision.

● Pretty baskets on each side of a traditional bow window differ in size and planting schemes. Nasturtiums and pelargoniums on the left link with petunias in the barrel below and contrast with fuchsias, petunias, trailing nepeta and ivy in the opposite basket.

● Strongly shaped planting suits an individual window. The spiky cordyline has been surrounded with holly, cyclamen, gold-tinged euonymus, ivy and silvery *Senecio maritima* all of which will survive the winter in a sheltered spot and continue to provide interesting foliage.

● A classic bay window with deep sills has the advantage of three separate positions for windowboxes. You could opt for a co-ordinated scheme or, as here, aim for three completely different planting arrangements of ivy, red pelargoniums and marigolds with lobelia and helichrysum.

● Sometimes delicate planting schemes can be the most effective, especially when you have taken into consideration the background – in this case an old brick and half-timbered building. Here a mix of the palest pink busy lizzies and mauve and white lobelia works well.

● White render makes an excellent backdrop for a traditional mix of pelargoniums, begonia and lobelia. The unusually positioned boxes above the window link well with the ground-level planting and the pristine, newly painted white lattice above and below.

● A cascading windowbox links ground floor and basement windows. Three pelargoniums – a double bright red (*Pelargonium hortorum* 'Gustave Emich'), a bi-coloured pink and a small white pelargonium – sit above purple verbena and deep pink 'Surfinia' (trailing petunia).

17

THINGS TO THINK ABOUT

Before you rush out and buy a basket or box and some colourful plants to fill it, there are a few things worth remembering. They could be called the four Ss – season, size, soil and site – all factors worth bearing in mind whether you are planting up your first basket or trying something completely new.

Season

It used to be assumed that hanging baskets and windowboxes were just for the warm summer months but now you will see colourful pansy balls throughout the autumn and early spring and wonderful winter windowboxes that are especially welcome when gardens are bare.

Evergreen foliage can be attractive in itself – with golden tones and berried plants adding extra brilliance. Later in the year, some plants may be discarded and flowering plants added.

• Be aware of the size of your house in proportion to the size of basket. Too small a basket, such as this one of pink and white diascia, looks lost, whereas a basket of the correct size and planting will enhance your home and appear to be in balance.

Size

Do bear in mind the size of your window when buying or making a windowbox. Those that are too small can look rather mean and out of place. The larger and deeper your box, the easier it will be to maintain healthy plants. A larger box can hold more soil and therefore retains more moisture when you water, thus avoiding one of the major problems, that of drying out.

Think about buying a basket a size larger than you had first planned – 30-cm (12 in) baskets are really only suitable for very small arrangements and will dry out very quickly indeed. A 35-cm basket (14 in) is a good general standard, while a 40-cm (16 in) basket will give you a full and professional-looking display. The larger baskets can be very heavy when the soil is wet so ensure that your fixings are strong and secure.

Soil

Some plants need a particular soil type to survive. Heathers, for example, like an acid soil and will quickly die in soil that is full of lime. Most plants are quite happy in a multi-purpose potting compost but it is worth checking, either with your garden centre or in the plants section at the back of this book (see page 104).

Some plants, such as alpines, need a well-drained soil which can be achieved by mixing in horticultural grit. If you are planting them in a

• A box of hot summer colour that thrives in a sunny spot: marguerites, marigolds, petunias, helichrysum, lobelia, pelargonium, flossflower and felicia all love the sun, whereas the fuchsias and busy lizzies would do equally well in semi-shade.

windowbox, place a layer of broken crocks or pebbles over the holes in the base of the box to ensure adequate drainage.

Most plants dislike sitting in water and if you are worried about overwatering it is worth layering charcoal in the base layer of soil to prevent mould and mildew. You will find further information about compost types on page 100.

Site

It is easy to assume that hanging baskets and windowboxes are best situated in a sunny spot, however many plants, such as busy lizzies, fuchsias and pansies, will flower happily in the shade and numerous evergreens will give a verdant display in shady spots all year round.

Success often depends on the position of the basket or box. Check whether plants prefer a sunny, shady or semi-shady position. (See page 104.)

• These pink and white ornamental cabbages and heathers create a living collage for the winter months but will not survive long without ericaceous (acidic) compost.

• Here the paler green of spotted laurel and the darker green of conifers form the basis of an attractive winter scheme – cyclamen will survive among the warmth of city buildings and are offset by silver *Artemisia absinthium* and variegated ivy.

WHERE TO HANG A BASKET

The most obvious place for a basket is by a doorway – and with good reason. It can be seen whenever you enter the house and will be enjoyed by neighbours and casual passersby.

However there are many other areas that benefit greatly from a colourful display of baskets. Fences and walls, sheds and garages all become attractive features when festooned with flowers and foliage.

You can make your own holders for baskets – such as the post with brackets and the trellis shown here. Or simply use standard brackets well fixed into the wall.

Consider where your basket will be most appreciated. A herb basket by the back door will be in easy reach and will bring the scent of aromatic herbs into your kitchen.

Try to plant according to the position of your basket. Choose sun-lovers for a sunny site and plants tolerant of shade for cooler spots.

Wherever your basket is to be hung, check that it is not going to hit anyone on the head. Baskets can be extremely heavy when full and well watered.

Do ensure that your basket is not going to be a nuisance to pedestrians – if it is going to hang over a pavement, set the fixings higher and use a rise and fall system for watering.

● Two rows of baskets along a fence disguise what could be a boring area of the garden and give it a totally different feel. *Lobelia erinus* in shades of purple, lilac, white and the less common, deep carmine 'Rosamund' vie for space with marigolds, pansies, alyssum and white petunias.

● Create a striking basket of pastel colour using one simple variety. Here busy lizzies (*Impatiens walleriana*) hung above a doorway combine tones of pink, white and lilac planted all round the basket to give a ball effect.

● Transform a dull brick wall with a trellis of hanging baskets. Here brilliant pelargoniums (*Pelargonium hortorum* 'Paul Crampel' and 'Queen of the Whites') are intermingled with petunias and marigolds underslung with red and blue lobelia interspersed with variegated ivies.

● Fuchsias and busy lizzies would thrive in a shady spot – such as under this tree – but lobelia requires some sunshine so the basket would need to be moved for some part of the day. Lilac, purple and masses of white lobelia combine to create a cool and delicate spherical basket.

● A fence post or purpose-made bracket holder creates a stunning area of the garden when holding two brimming hanging baskets. Variegated petunias, white alyssum, pelargoniums, nasturtiums and marigolds make a show when mingled with mixed shades of lobelia.

● Make the entrance to your house welcoming with brimming baskets of colour hung on each side of the door. Delicate pink shades of tobacco plant, lobelia and pale green helichrysum tone with the stronger pinks of 'Surfinia', busy lizzie and fuchsia in the adjacent basket.

21

• Symmetrical baskets of trailing ivy-leaf pelargoniums (*Pelargonium peltatum* 'Galilee'). To create a spherical effect, two baskets have been planted separately and then wired together. This shows how baskets can contrast effectively with your wall colour, rather than toning in.

• It's tempting to echo the colours of your garden in your windowboxes but here a cool planting scheme of green foliage would simply fade into obscurity. Instead, a bright arrangement of marigolds, busy lizzies and petunias provides a refreshing contrast.

• A striking purple and stained-glass door is set off to perfection with a hanging basket of petunias, pelargoniums and lobelia, with trailing ivy, in harmonious shades of pink, green and lilac, backed by rambling clematis bearing purple flowers that match the shade of the door.

• Five pots of vibrant zinnias have extra impact when used *en masse* between tomato-red window shutters. Do not be afraid to employ bold blocks of colour. Try veering away from standard arrangements of pastel colours and you are likely to be surprised and delighted with the results.

COLOUR BALANCE

From co-ordination to creative contrast, the plants you use in your boxes and baskets should be chosen carefully. Plan them to link with your house or garden and the result will be tastefully artistic.

The colours you choose for your planting schemes are your own personal area of design, even on such a small scale, so it is worth trying to imagine the effects you hope to achieve rather than just picking up a random assortment of plants at your garden centre and hoping that they will all work together 'somehow'.

First, look at the exterior of your home. Are there colours you can pick up on, e.g. in the door or window frames? Are there plants in the bed below the window, which you would like to echo in your windowbox or hanging basket?

This is not to say that a mixed selection of plants cannot look particularly effective. Indeed, most baskets that you will see contain a mixture of colours. By studying other baskets, you will see that some of the most effective are those that have been planned to co-ordinate with, or make a contrast to, the house, another windowbox or each other.

Plan ahead. If you think your paintwork or render needs freshening up, do it *before* you hang baskets or fix boxes. Of course, if you are thinking of repainting, you can always make your new paintwork match your boxes and baskets.

• A cascading basket of pendulous fuchsias and Swedish ivy echoes and emphasises the pink wall. Here hybrid petunias, pelargoniums and variegated pinks on the windowsills link with the healthy hydrangea and miniature roses below to stunning effect.

• Numerous shades of yellow and orange plants work well together and contrast attractively here with the green foliage and paintwork. Dahlias, marigolds, pansies and celosia co-ordinate beautifully with variegated ivies, helichrysum and the rudbeckia and sunflowers below.

HOT COLOURS BRIGHT IDEAS

Make the most of nature's brilliance with a basket or windowbox in vibrant colours that cheer and inspire. Choose from a profusion of begonias to a cascade of mixed summer colour.

● An array of these feather duster plants would brighten up any corner. Commonly known as 'Prince of Wales feathers' (*Celosia amaranthaceae*) they come in red, pink, yellow and salmon and look amusingly pert with their crested blooms. They do not grow very tall so are ideal for windowboxes.

● A striking combination of marigolds, monkey flower, chrysanthemums, pelargoniums and petunias. Take a closer look to spot the blues of felicia and campanula, the white marguerites and deep red lobelia – the details which give the arrangement depth.

M any of the plants that enjoy the heat of summer come in a range of hot and sultry colours. From begonias and the fiery feather dusters of celosia, to luminous marigolds and bright pelargoniums, their brilliance proclaims that summer has arrived at last.

Many daisy-like plants, including Cape marigold (*Dimorphotheca*), gazanias, zinnias and helichrysum, open up in brilliant sunshine. Others that particularly enjoy direct light and warmth are petunias, pinks, miniature roses and verbena. Direct sunlight can, of course, be terribly fierce and drying. Some plants will need watering more than once a day and perhaps moving to a shady spot for a few hours to avoid the worst of the sun's rays.

Succulent plants, such as portulaca and flowering cacti, are designed to survive well in hot conditions, storing water in their fleshy leaves.

Plants sited in very hot places will need plenty of water. Avoid getting water on leaves or petals as the tiny drops of water act like magnifying glasses in strong sunlight and will cause the leaves or petals to burn.

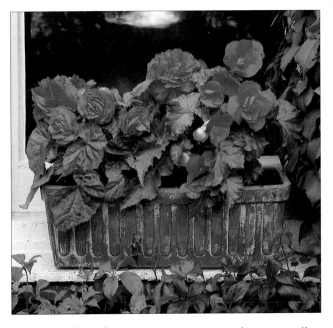

● For the first bright, heartwarming colours of the year, you can't fail to please with ranunculus – wonderful peony-like plants from the buttercup family. These are available from early spring in rich single colours and more delicate whites with pink edging and will flower until late summer.

● In return for rich, moist potting compost, begonias will reward you with vibrant colour. Choose the smaller blooms of the low-growing varieties, such as *Begonia multiflora*, for windowboxes and take care not to plant out until the frosts are over. Here, a terracotta pot adds to the warm effect.

● The apricot yellow of a pendulous begonia is given extra warmth by the proximity of a double pink busy lizzie. Purple brachycome and pale pink lobelia combine with a deep red, clustered fuchsia (*F.* 'Thalia') to make this a harmoniously colourful basket.

● Luminous trailing begonias (*Begonia semperflorens*), French marigolds (*Tagetes patula* 'Goldfinch') and large clusters of purple lobelia (*Lobelia erinus* 'Crystal Palace') combine to provide an eyecatching windowbox that will remain a profusion of colour throughout the summer.

● Create a miniature garden of soft colours in a windowbox. A tiny privet (*Ligustrum*) sits beside a trellis 'fence'. Miniature roses grow among pelargoniums and parsley. Trailing bugle (*Ajuga*) and euonymus soften the line of the box.

● Delicate shades of an unusual woolly lavender (*Lavandula lanata*) combine with the cool greens and creams of variegated sage, ivy and a small-leaved helichrysum (*H.* 'Roundabout') to create a windowbox that would give off a delicious scent when brushed past.

COOL CREATIONS

Aim for subtle, calming colours – greens, yellows, pinks and whites – for baskets and windowboxes that suggest peace and tranquillity. Blend them together for a harmonious scheme, choosing a range of delicate shades from the same colour palette.

In contrast to many of the fiery schemes of high summer, it can be particularly refreshing to cast your eye over something a little more subtle. There are many wonderful foliage plants which tend to be ignored or used solely as a backdrop. However, when used together, these can look sophisticated and quite different in a cool, quiet way.

Many herbs have an interesting leaf shape which makes them useful both artistically and for culinary purposes. Flowering thyme, the soft 'rabbit ears' of sage, and the feathery foliage of fennel give textured appeal as well as the added bonus of a fragrance wafting through the air.

Most of the silver-leaved plants, including cineraria or dusty miller (*Senecio*) need more sun to keep their colour than might be imagined, but are particularly rewarding.

Some miniature roses can be obtained in very sweet, soft colours, as can a whole range of wildflowers.

- The arching stems of this attractive silver-leafed chamomile (*Anthemis punctata*) reach skywards and create an attractively feathered hanging basket. An upright fuchsia (*F.* 'Sunray') and dusty miller (*Senecio maritima cirrhus*) keep the scheme within similar cool tones.

- In contrast to many brightly coloured windowboxes, the soft yellows and whites of pansies, marguerites and busy lizzies and the subtle blues of felicia and spurred *Diascia cordata* offer a refreshingly natural look. These plants would enjoy a position in semi-shade.

- For a simple but effective winter windowbox, purple cineraria (*Senecio hybridus*) surrounded by evergreen foliage – laurel, spotted laurel and a star-shaped ivy (*Hedera helix* 'Pittsburgh') – makes a striking combination. The bold cineraria flowers for many winter months.

- For an interesting foliage basket that also produces pale blue flowers from mid-spring to early summer, bugle (*Ajuga reptans* 'Burgundy Glow') is a good choice. The leaves are wine red with white and pink shading and this evergreen alpine will grow happily in sun or deep shade.

27

• Many plants that may appear too tall for windowboxes also come in dwarf varieties. These blue dwarf delphiniums look particularly attractive against a lemon-washed wall with the green of the foliage echoed in the windowbox. They flower from late spring to early summer.

• Miniature tête à tête daffodils herald the arrival of spring, their strong, fresh, yellow heads nodding in the breeze against verdant standard and attractively variegated ivies. Plant the ivies in autumn with daffodil bulbs below and winter pansies above.

• A mass of trailing pink pelargoniums (*Pelargonium* 'Mini Cascade') provides welcome colour on a smart city street. The black of the door and shutters contrasts sharply with the soft pinks of the hanging basket. Pelargoniums are ideal for hanging baskets as they survive with little water.

• An ever-popular mix of pendulous fuchsia, begonia and trailing pelargonium will win favour through being prolific and striking, although not without some effort. Fuchsias are particularly demanding of water. This basket is suitable for a semi-shady position.

SINGLE-COLOUR PLANTING

For baskets and windowboxes with the greatest impact, it is hard to better the effect of single-colour planting. Hanging balls or overflowing windowboxes of one flower or colour type never fail to catch the eye.

It is extremely easy to push a trolley around a nursery or garden centre picking up trays of plants which catch your eye, perhaps even buying two or three new varieties if you are feeling adventurous. The results, however, may not always be as impressive as you might hope. Take a look in other trolleys and you will see that some people are planning an all-blue scheme or one of white and green only. Even before planting up, you can see how well colours of a similar hue work together, while a mixture can look garish and jumbled.

Take a tip from the experts and plan your scheme before you venture out. Make notes from year to year of successful and rewarding schemes and keep the plant tags to remind you. From sunny yellow daffodils with simple green foliage to an all-white daisy, or all-blue lobelia, ball, there are a myriad ways to use a group of plants within one area of the colour palette. The results can be most effective.

● For a strikingly pretty ball of daisies, follow the planting instructions for the pansy ball on page 78. If plug plants are not available simply make larger holes for more mature plants. The marguerites will fill out and, with regular deadheading, will bloom all summer long.

● A wicker hamper makes an attractive windowbox when lined with slit plastic to prevent compost from leaking out. Here a mass of orange chrysanthemums provides a block of warm colour that will flower from late summer to early autumn in a sunny spot.

● Green and white schemes look effective – clean and modern, romantically soft and pretty – especially when many plants are used. Here hybrid busy lizzies, pinks (*Dianthus* 'Snowflake'), forget-me-not (*Myosotis* 'White Ball'), ivy and plectranthus are artistically combined.

● You can grow herbs on a sunny windowsill but this basket would need to spend some time outside too. Sorrel, parsley, mint, chives and thyme would cater for many of your cooking requirements and the mingled trailing foliage looks particularly attractive.

● This relatively new fuchsia variety, *Fuchsia* 'Autumnale', has wonderful leaf colouring and creates enough foliage interest to make a striking hanging basket on its own. However, it also produces bright pink flowers in summer and autumn and enjoys a shady position.

● As an alternative to ivy, plectranthus is rapidly gaining in popularity for both hanging baskets and windowboxes. Its attractive variegated leaf and natural trailing habit make it an ideal backdrop to many planting schemes. Plectranthus also looks quite dramatic when used alone.

SHADES OF GREEN

Rethink your attitude towards foliage schemes – the subtleties of leaf structure can be more fascinating than the most colourful planting arrangement.

When planning a hanging basket or windowbox, many of us instinctively opt for the latest trend in colours – recently blue, pink and purple have had a revival, whereas ten years ago it was orange and yellow. Looking at some of the windowboxes used by commercial properties, however, such as hotels, shops and offices, proves that there are valuable lessons to be learnt. Here a backdrop of evergreens, such as conifers and ivies, is used all year round, interplanted with polyanthus and pansies in spring, pelargoniums and begonias in summer, chrysanthemums in autumn and cineraria in winter, all prolific-flowering plants of their season, which look good against a green backdrop.

It is unfair to place foliage plants in the sole role of backdrop to flowering planting schemes, however, as many non-flowering plants are very rewarding in their own right.

From the luxuriant colours of coleus to the deep burgundy brown of Japanese maple (*Acer palmatum*) there are innumerable foliage plants which go extremely well together or will create an unusual hanging basket when used entirely alone.

● A multitude of plants have been chosen here, particularly for their unusual foliage. From beetroot to nasturtiums, zonal pelargoniums to spurge, pick-a-back plant (*Tolmiea*) to periwinkle, the different leaf structures look wonderful when grouped in a windowbox.

● For an attractive trug of green foliage plants that is also useful, try keeping herbs on a windowsill near the kitchen door. Flowering thyme, variegated sage, curled parsley and tarragon jostle happily for space and will give an aromatic bonus too when carried on the warm summer air.

SINGLE PLANT TYPES OR SPECIES

Simplify your ideas and you will be surprised by the results. Individual plant schemes have a great deal of poise and horticultural panache.

While you can achieve a planting scheme of great impact by using a number of different plants within one range of colour, the most striking baskets and windowboxes, especially from a distance, are those containing a single species, variety or plant type.

Whether you choose a windowbox of begonias or a basket of busy lizzies, the results are likely to be impressive. Check through our pointers on pages 18 and 19 to ensure that you have taken into account the four Ss – site, season, soil and situation. Busy lizzies will thrive in a shady spot but some plants need more careful siting. Different varieties of pansies bloom happily throughout the seasons but not all plants are so happy all year round. Some plants, such as the hydrangeas shown here, are rarely seen in baskets, perhaps because they require ericaceous (lime-free) compost or large amounts of water and possibly because they can grow fairly large, so that most people think of them as a garden shrub.

The easiest single plant types to grow must be pelargoniums, more varieties of which are being bred all the time. As single planting schemes, they are hard to better.

● Pansy balls make rewarding hanging baskets, bringing bright colour to cheer the winter months, and then again through spring and summer. There are numerous varieties available including this cheerful mixture (*Viola* 'Universal' mixed). (Follow the instructions on page 78.)

● Bold pelargoniums (*Pelargonium hortorum* 'Red Elite') brighten the grey brick of a typical town house. Pelargoniums flower best in a sunny spot and are easy to grow as they can survive with less water than many plants, although occasional feeding will boost the display.

● Linking two baskets, one hanging, one used on a windowsill, with a similar colour scheme, looks effective without being ostentatious. The ball of pink tradescantia – a recently developed plant – harmonises well with the chrysanthemums – yet both have individual character.

● Create a stunning spherical basket using the colour spectrum of one single species. Here busy lizzie (*Impatiens walleriana*) has been used to great effect by combining subtle tones of pink, white and lilac planted through the basket to give all-round growth.

● Enjoy a blue mophead hydrangea at close quarters by siting it in a windowbox with variegated ivies. You can buy the ericaceous compost which it needs to keep its colour or convert multi-purpose compost by adding a liquid solution, using powders available from garden centres.

● The palette of pink, white and purple shades found in these heathers (*Erica cineraria* 'Moonstone White', *E. vagans* 'Mrs D.F. Maxwell' and *Calluna vulgaris* 'Silver Knight') combines well in a windowsill trug. Heathers require ericaceous compost and moist conditions.

PLANTING AND PLANTING DESIGNS

Gardening on the small scale presented by windowboxes and hanging baskets is the perfect opportunity to try out all sorts of planting schemes that you might not otherwise attempt.

From herb gardens to scented baskets, this is your chance to try out new arrangements with a specific theme in mind. Alpines, for instance, can soon be lost in a larger bed but are easy to appreciate at eye level. Also, the free-draining environment that they most appreciate can readily be created.

You may have thought it would be fun to make a pansy ball but were not quite sure how to go about it. The clear, step-by-step instructions given on page 78 will make the whole process less daunting.

Rather than producing just a simple basket of mixed flowers in summer, it is worth considering year-round planting schemes. Winter evergreens can be underplanted with spring bulbs and then added to for colourful summer arrangements.

Edible plants in baskets and windowboxes, such as strawberries and tomatoes, are ideal for those of us with little space. Their early flowers make them an attractive feature even before the fruits appear.

Whatever your interest, there are planting schemes on the following pages to inspire you – if you have always yearned for a wildflower garden or simply need to fill a shady corner, browse through these pages and you will find schemes for all sites and seasons.

MAKING A WINDOWBOX

Begin by measuring and marking the position of the angle brackets, as shown. With the bradawl make holes, where marked, for each set of four screws. Insert the screws – an electric screwdriver makes the job much quicker. Ensure that the last piece you add is a long side and screw the brackets to this before fixing it to the box as it can be fiddly screwing both angles of the last brackets directly into the box.

Lime is dangerous to work with as it can cause caustic burns unless you wear thick gloves. If you do choose to use powdered lime, you will need to add water until you have a runny liquid. A similar effect can be achieved using white emulsion.

You may need to water the paint down until it is the consistency of single cream. Apply to all areas of the box, except the base. When dry, use the wire brush to remove paint until you are happy with the result. A certain amount of woodgrain should show through.

YOU WILL NEED

8 × 5 cm (3 × 2 in) stainless steel angle brackets
3 pieces timber 15 × 75 cm
(6 × 30 in)
2 pieces timber 15 × 15 cm
(6 × 6 in)
32 × 1 cm flat-head screws
tape measure · pencil
screwdriver · bradawl

1 Follow the instructions in the main text for assembling the windowbox. Remember to drill holes in the base for drainage. Three holes at regular intervals should be sufficient for this size of box. Increase the number if you are making a larger box.

2 If you are staining the box, rub in woodstain using a soft cloth. We chose a soft yellow to enhance our bronze stars and silver moon stencils but almost any shade of brown or green would be certain of complementing your floral arrangement.

3 Old, roughened timber is often best for showing off a limed effect. You will probably still need to rough up the grain with a wire brush, deepening the grooves along the straight of the grain. Some woodgrain should show through.

4 You can then stencil the limed trough using your chosen design, or plant it in its natural state without any further ornamentation. A coat of clear matt varnish will ensure that your limed effect and stencil does not wash off in the rain.

Handpainted windowboxes and pots with limed and stencilled finishes.

Stencilling

Plastic stencils are widely available in craft shops or you can make your own using a scalpel and stencil card. Quick-drying stencil paints are available but thick household emulsions can work just as well on wooden windowboxes as long as a final coat of clear matt varnish is put on to seal in your design. If you use exterior paints, this will not be necessary.

You may have leftover household paints which you can use or might be able to obtain small sample pots that fit your intended scheme. Small pots of enamel paints in primary colours, and metallics intended for toy painting are also suitable.

Many gardeners have artistic leanings and you may be inspired to paint your own container, such as the watering can shown here. First paint your container in a base colour and allow it to dry completely. Then, after sketching your idea on paper, transfer it to the metal medium using suitable paints. For beginners, an abstract leaf shape would be easier than the scene shown here of swans on a lake. If this is the first time you have painted pots and containers, do not be too ambitious with your first attempts.

1 Using either plastic or terracotta pots, fix on your stencil with masking tape and apply the paint using a stencil brush. If stencilling a wooden windowbox, paint it in your base colour and allow it to dry thoroughly overnight.

2 If the paint tends to seep beneath the stencil on a plastic pot, it may be easier to outline the design using a chinagraph pencil, then remove the stencil and infill with enamel paints using the smaller paintbrush.

3 You may wish to use just part of a larger stencil to create a co-ordinating theme. Bold blocks of primary colours work well, giving the effect of barge painting. Fine detail will only be seen close up so decide in advance where to put the pot.

YOU WILL NEED

1 litre (1¾ pt) base colour exterior paint – matt, silk or gloss (for box) · a stencil masking tape · chinagraph pencil · enamel or gloss paints stencil or thick-headed brushes fine brush for detailed work

QUICK TIPS

● Choose stencils that give bright blocks of colour. These will look very effective from a distance.

● If paint runs beneath stencils on a plastic pot, outline the design in chinagraph pencil and then paint this.

● Do not be too ambitious with your first attempts unless you are sure of your artistic skills.

● If painting a windowbox, apply a painted base coat of one colour and allow this to dry overnight. Otherwise the stencil may smudge.

Springtime primulas in an ethnic, stencilled windowbox with handpainted bargeware pots and a watering can.

PLANTING

Step by Step to Planting a Windowbox

Just like hanging baskets, windowboxes have a tendency to dry out so some of these steps are specifically intended to counteract this problem.

The planting scheme itself can be varied to suit almost any colours you have in mind – there are plenty of ideas throughout the book – but we thought these bright oranges and blues made a refreshing change from more traditional colours. Hydrangeas make particularly good container plants as long as the soil is ericaceous (acidic not alkaline) and they are kept well watered.

Tip: Charcoal scattered in the base will prevent container plants from becoming mildewed through overwatering.

YOU WILL NEED

a windowbox, e.g. wood, stone, plastic, terracotta
10 kg (22 lb) ericaceous compost
broken crocks or pebbles for base
plastic for lining
water-retaining granules
fertiliser granules
8 French marigolds · 6 African marigolds · 10 petunia
1 scabious · 1 hydrangea
a hand-operated or electric drill

1 Provide drainage holes in the base of the box – one every 15 cm (6 in). Then cover the base inside with crocks or pebbles to prevent soil from leaching out. A plastic lining or pre-formed liner will prevent a wooden box bowing through damp.

2 Fill to one-third with compost (for most plants a multi-purpose variety is adequate but the hydrangea will need ericaceous compost) adding a few handfuls of water-retaining granules. Sprinkle in the fertiliser.

3 Test run the position of the plants while still in their pots, then insert the hydrangea. Place the medium-sized scabious on the left. Add the African and French marigolds and infill with petunias. Fill with compost and water in.

1 *French marigolds*
2 *African marigolds*
3 *petunia*
4 *scabious*
5 *hydrangea*

Plant a basic windowbox with a vibrant purple and orange theme using marigolds and a hydrangea.

Planting a Basic Hanging Basket

Here we aim to give you a 'recipe' so that you can recreate the colourful summer basket opposite. Clear step-by-step photographs and instructions are provided, although they do not need to be followed to the letter. These plants are all popular for container gardening. However, should a particular plant be unavailable, your garden centre will advise you of a suitable substitute.

We have used quite a large basket as the 26- and 30-cm (10 and 12 in) versions hold too little compost and tend to dry out quickly. Lack of water is the most common reason for unsuccessful hanging baskets. A liner made of plastic, fibrous matting or foam will help to retain water. 'Self-watering' baskets are available, with a reservoir of water in the base, but these are generally made of plastic so plants cannot be pushed through the sides.

YOU WILL NEED

a plastic-coated wire basket
36 cm (14 in) in diameter
2 kg (4½ lb) bag of moss
5 kg (11 lb) potting compost
fibrous/foam liner (optional) or
plastic cut to fit
1 trailing begonia
1 pelargonium · 1 pot verbena
1 pink busy lizzie
3 purple petunias
1 pot *Bidens aurea*
1 rock rose (*heliantheum*)
lobelia or pansies
watering can · trowel

1 First assemble your 'ingredients'. You may find it easier to put your basket on a bucket. Then plan the arrangement, with the tallest plants to the rear and the smallest, trailing plants around the edges or inserted from below.

2 Line the basket with the moss, arranging it to cover the entire surface. Add the fibrous, paper or foam liner, cutting holes for lower planting if the liner allows. Half-fill with compost. Remove plants from pots with care to avoid root damage.

3 Plant the begonia and pelargonium in the centre. Thread lobelia and *Bidens aurea* roots into the base from the outside. Add the other plants, then fill up with potting compost right to the brim. Firm the plants and water well.

1 *begonia*
2 *pelargonium*
3 *verbena*
4 *busy lizzie*
5 *petunia*
6 Bidens area
7 *lobelia*
8 *rock rose*

A basket of mixed summer flowers – begonia, petunia, verbena, busy lizzie, pelargonium and *Bidens aurea*.

Planting a Wall-mounted Half-basket

Wall-mounted baskets give a plain wall life and colour. They take up less space than hanging baskets and generally hold fewer plants. Because less compost is needed, however, they are more prone to drying out and need careful attention and regular watering.

Take into consideration the aspect of your wall when choosing plants. If it is a shady spot, you will find that pelargoniums will flower very little – opt for busy lizzies or fuchsias instead. A hot spot could make an ideal site for nasturtiums or other sun-loving plants.

Wall fixings need to be strong and secure. A full half-basket can be very heavy and plants will be damaged should it fall.

It is worth lining the whole of the basket with polythene, especially the back, to prevent marks on your wall if you remove the basket during the winter.

YOU WILL NEED

a cast-iron or plastic-coated wire half-basket 36 cm (14 in) in diameter
black plastic
5 kg (11 lb) potting compost
2 kg (4½ lb) bag of moss
2 pelargoniums – one trailing, one upright · Swedish ivy (*Nepeta*) · 6 lobelia · 6 busy lizzie (*Impatiens*) · 1 creeping jenny (*Lysimachia nummularia*) · 1 red mimulus · 1 purple brachycome

1 Line the basket with black plastic, ensuring the back wall is well protected. Fill with moss in front of the plastic, with the greenest part outermost, right up and over the top edge. Fill one-third with potting compost.

2 Sprinkle in granular fertiliser and add a further third of compost. Starting at one side, make cuts through the plastic liner with scissors and insert the busy lizzie and lobelia, alternately, halfway down the basket to cover the sides.

3 Test your plan by placing the plants in the basket still in their pots. Place the upright pelargonium in the centre and the trailing plants to the sides, with the Swedish ivy at the centre front. Plant up the basket and firm the plants in.

1 *Swedish ivy*
2 *lobelia*
3 *busy lizzie*
4 *creeping jenny*
5 *mimulus*
6 *brachycome*
7 *pelargonium*

A colourful mix of pelargoniums, monkey flower and purple brachycome, with trailing lobelia and Swedish ivy.

SPRING FLOWERS
Easter Windowbox

The best known spring-flowering bulbs – daffodils, tulips, grape hyacinths, iris and crocus – have earned their popularity by being hardy enough to withstand the cold winds and rain of early spring and looking bright and colourful at a time of year when our gardens are only just coming into bud. However, many lesser-known bulbs are also worth trying, from the bell-like blue scillas to anemones.

As many spring bulbs, including crocus, daffodils and tulips, flower a few weeks after each other, many gardeners suggest surface planting with pansies or primulas in spring to give a constant display through which the bulbs can grow.

Our colourful windowbox is quite simple to plant, using trailing ivies, box and rosemary as a foliage base, with blue grape hyacinths underplanted in autumn and primula and polyanthus in yellow, pink and purple added later.

YOU WILL NEED

1 windowbox about 75 cm (30 in) long and 15 cm (6 in) deep
broken crocks or pebbles
multi-purpose potting compost
2 trailing ivies (*Hedera*)
2 pieces of green foliage (e.g. rosemary, box)
3 primulas · 2 purple polyanthus · 25–30 grape hyacinth bulbs (*Muscari*)

1 Arrange broken crocks to cover the drainage holes in the base of your windowbox. Fill the box to just below the rim with potting compost and plant the grape hyacinth bulbs in clumps 3 cm (1 in) below the surface in mid to late autumn.

2 Plant up with the foliage to the rear and the ivies trailing over the front and sides. Infill with polyanthus and primulas as soon as you can find them, leaving space for the grape hyacinths to push through. Water the compost until it is damp but not waterlogged.

QUICK TIPS

• Drill holes in plastic troughs for drainage if none exist. Cover with crocks or pebbles and fill to just below the brim with compost.
• Plant bulbs in rows or clusters, with the largest bulbs lowest. Cover with potting compost, water in and leave in a shady spot until late winter, keeping the soil moist. Then move to a sunny spot to encourage flowering.
• Add charcoal to prevent bulbs rotting.

1 *grape hyacinth*
2 *ivy*
3 *green foliage*
4 *primula*
5 *polyanthus*

Celebrate the coming of spring with blue grape hyacinths, fresh green rosemary and bright primulas.

Planting a Spring Hanging Basket

After the dull dark days of winter, it is cheering to see bulbs bursting into life, especially if you can position them in a basket near your front door.

If you intend using bulbs, you need to start planning in early autumn and planting in mid-autumn. Choose dwarf varieties for windowboxes where possible or you may find that the stems grow too long and the plants droop or become too lanky and make the basket look uneven.

Alternatively, a visit to your local garden centre in early to mid-spring can supply you with a colourful display of ready-grown bulbs that are hardy enough to withstand frosts and strong winds.

We chose a fairly traditional yellow mixture of tête à tête narcissi, dwarf tulips, a cowslip and a large primrose and added colour with pink and red daisies (*Bellis*) and clumps of grape hyacinth and scilla with its delicate, blue, star-shaped flowers.

YOU WILL NEED

a basket approximately 50 cm (20 in) in diameter
thick plastic for liner
multi-purpose potting
compost · moss
1 cowslip (*Primula veris*)
tête à tête narcissi · 2 dwarf
tulips · 2 daisies (*Bellis*)
1 grape hyacinth (*Muscari*)
1 *Scilla sibirica* · 2 primroses
(*Primula*)
1 spurge (*Euphorbia*)

1 Gather your ingredients. Choose a basket with an interesting shape. Remember that it must be deep enough to hold the compost and must have a very strong handle as it will be heavy when filled with fully grown plants and wet compost.

2 Line the basket with moss then cut the plastic to shape for the liner. (Part of a compost bag will do.) Make slits to ensure adequate drainage and fill to two-thirds with potting compost. Decide which is to be the front of your basket.

3 Start by placing the taller plants at the back. The cowslip, grape hyacinth and scilla will add central colour. Infill with primroses and daisies at the front. Add extra compost where required and water in well.

1 cowslip
2 tête à tête narcissi
3 tulip
4 daisy
5 grape hyacinth
6 scilla
7 primrose
8 spurge

Create a pink, white and yellow theme with *Bellis* daisies, tête à tête daffodils and dwarf tulips.

HERBS

While a traditional herb garden can take up a great deal of space in a valuable sunny area of the garden, a windowbox or hanging basket takes up very little room and can be positioned right outside the kitchen door.

The sometimes pungent scent given off by herbs can remind one of the Mediterranean, from where many culinary herbs originate. Perhaps because of their origins, most herbs prefer a sunny spot and gritty, free-draining soil.

Few of us appreciate how pretty the foliage of a selection of herbs can be until we plant them together.

A Herb Windowbox

For a small and stylish windowbox that you can keep close at hand on a kitchen windowsill, a simple metal container such as this is ideal. Most herbs need a sunny situation to do well and this box would do equally well outside your kitchen door if conditions are right. We have used five of the most popular herbs.

YOU WILL NEED

a container, 30–50 cm (12–20 in) long in metal, plastic or terracotta
1 chive (*Allium schoenoprasum*)
1 parsley (*Petroselinum*)
1 thyme (*Thymus*)
1 lemon balm (*Melissa officinalis*)
1 mint (*Mentha*)
crocks · medium potting mixture – half-grit half-potting compost

---

1 Before you begin to plant them, test out the position of the plants first, keeping them in their pots, to judge where you wish them to trail and how the leaf colours work best together. Place the crocks in the base and fill with gritted compost.

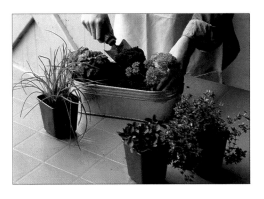

2 Plant the herbs, teasing the roots out gently to help them to acclimatise quickly. Train them to trail over the sides of the container if you wish. Water in, taking care not to overwater. Cut herbs often to promote bushy growth.

QUICK TIPS
● Try to choose a spot that will make it easy for you to snip the herbs when preparing a meal.
● If you are using the windowbox inside, you will not need drainage holes but you will have to be careful when watering to ensure that the soil does not become waterlogged.
● Remove flowerheads from chives etc. to promote leaf growth.

1 *chives*
2 *parsley*
3 *thyme*
4 *lemon balm*
5 *mint*

Keep basic herbs, such as parsely, chives, thyme and mint, close at hand on your kitchen windowsill.

A Herb Cooking Guide

Chives: best used at the end of cooking. Snip over soups and sauces, mix with cream cheese over jacket potatoes.

Fennel: the stalk and leaves taste of aniseed and are good in tomato and fish sauces.

Mint: mostly used for mint sauce for lamb and with new potatoes. Also in tea.

Parsley: useful as an edible garnish, in stocks and to freshen breath. Useful in sauces for fish, ham and egg. Freezes well.

Sorrel: a few handfuls of the leaves (40 g or 1½ oz) are enough for a delicious soup. Tastes like spinach.

Tarragon: a few sprigs for bearnaise sauce or in wine vinegar for salad dressings.

Thyme: chopped in salad dressings – one teaspoon. Or little sprigs in stocks and casseroles – especially beef. Dries well.

A Herb Basket

YOU WILL NEED

2 fennel plants (*Foeniculum vulgare*)
1 plant each of sorrel (*Rumex*)
parsley (*Petroselinum*)
mint (*Mentha*)
thyme (*Thymus*)
chives (*Allium schoenoprasum*)
French tarragon
(*Artemisia dracunculus*)
sage (*Salvia*)
potting compost
horticultural grit

1 A plastic-lined wicker basket is ideal for an arrangement of herbs as long as you make a few slits in the plastic before filling to allow drainage. A ratio of about half grit and half compost gives the sort of free draining environment herbs prefer.

2 Start by planting the taller sorrel and fennel in the centre to the rear then adding the chives, mint, tarragon and parsley around the edges. Keep the compost moist but not soggy – the grit should ensure that the compost is well drained.

QUICK TIPS
● Always used a free-draining compost – mix half grit and half potting compost.
● Herbs enjoy a hot and sunny spot.
● Feed weekly during the summer months.
● Most plants will die off and need replacing next spring.
● You could keep your herb basket hanging in the kitchen once it is well established. Herbs enjoy sunshine though, so hang it outside occasionally in a sunny spot.
● Do not worry if the herbs dry out a little they will revive if trimmed and watered.
● Fennel grows to about 60 cm (2 ft) tall so only plant it if you have enough room.

1 *fennel*
2 *sorrel*
3 *parsley*
4 *mint*
5 *thyme*
6 *chives*
7 *French tarragon*
8 *sage*

Appreciate the textures and fragrance of Mediterranean herbs in a basket near your door.

Tomato and Lettuce Windowbox

As lettuce hearts up in around ten days, you will find you can pick them and replace them with smaller plants while waiting for the tomatoes to grow and ripen – around six to ten weeks, depending on the amount of light and warmth they receive.

Tomatoes are prone to aphids and may need spraying occasionally. If they appear to be wilting, ensure that they have enough water. You will need to pinch out trusses – wherever a new little stem grows directly between two stems – to prevent the plant from producing only tiny tomatoes.

Tumbler tomatoes will give a bushy trailing tomato that will break the line of the box and does not need pinching out. Otherwise opt for Totem – a compact, upright variety that will not grow too tall.

For lettuce, Cos is useful as an upright variety for infilling between tomato plants, otherwise Little Gem would be good or even the red-tinged Lollo Rosso.

YOU WILL NEED

2 tomato plants, Tumbler or
Totem
3 Cos lettuce
a windowbox around 60 cm
(2 ft) long
rich potting compost
water-retaining gel pellets
(optional)
slow-release fertiliser granules
(optional)

---

1 Three lettuce and two tomato plants will give a good yield. Drill holes in the base of your windowbox if there are none already. Line the base with crocks or pebbles for drainage, then fill to the brim with rich potting compost.

2 You can add slow-release fertiliser and water-retaining gel pellets at this stage – scattered about halfway down. Remove the plants from their pots, teasing the roots out gently. Plant alternately, with lettuces at the sides and centre.

3 Water in well. Make sure the compost covers the roots well. Firm it down a little and add more if necessary as it will sink with watering. Do not crowd the box with more plants as they require a lot of nutrients to produce a good crop.

QUICK TIPS

• Tomatoes need regular feeding and watering. Feed weekly with a liquid tomato fertiliser. Water twice daily in warm or windy weather. Spray to deter pests if necessary.
• Tumbler tomatoes are good for hanging baskets and boxes as they spill naturally over the sides and trail prettily. The tomatoes are also fairly small, sweet and juicy.
• Ensure the root ball of the tomato plant is well below the compost level to prevent drying out. Water in well.

Experiment with salad vegetables to produce a windowbox full of colour and with edible results.

A Strawberry Basket

A strawberry basket will bring delicious results and, with its white flowers and lustrous green foliage, will look attractive while you wait for it to bear fruit.

Ask the advice of your nursery or garden centre when choosing plants. You are looking for varieties with smaller leaves than many grown in vegetable plots, which produce a large crop of fruit.

All standard strawberry plants have pretty white flowers before they are pollinated; some have variegated foliage. Those with pink flowers look particularly pretty but some are not renowned for sweet-tasting fruit. Those used here, called *Fragaria* 'Strawberries and Cream' are, however, delicious.

Early planting, say, in mid to late spring, will give you a first strawberry crop in early summer, with another later in the season. To avoid frosts, you may wish to keep your basket in a greenhouse but do keep the door open on warm days to allow bees to enter and pollinate the flowers or else they will not produce fruit. An alternative is to wrap your basket in frost-proof fleece at night during the early part of the year. (This is available by the metre from many garden centres.) You will also find a few metres of this fleece invaluable for covering other baskets and boxes.

YOU WILL NEED

34-cm (14 in) wire basket
5 strawberry plants
moss
rich potting compost

1 Line your basket with moss. Bringing the moss up and over the brim will hide the wire. Fill with rich compost until it is level with the top and, if possible, add a season-long fertiliser. Check that this is suitable for fruit when you buy it.

2 Remove the plants from the pots and tease the roots out to encourage them to take quickly. Arrange them at angles all around the basket when planting so that some will trail. If you can, plant some through the sides and base. Then water in well.

QUICK TIPS

• A strawberry basket needs a rich potting compost, regular feeding and a sunny position.
• Water when the compost is dry but not too frequently as strawberries are particularly prone to mildew.
• Trim off any runners as the plant's energy will then be used to produce larger and sweeter fruit.
• Immediately after picking the fruit, cut off the leaves to about 7.5 cm (3 in) above the crown.
• Look out for Perpetual (Remontant) varieties as these have a long fruiting season, beginning in early summer and then fruiting again in late summer. Other varieties may only fruit once a year.
• Guard against damage by squirrels and birds by covering with fine-mesh plastic net while the fruit is forming.
• Pick the ripe strawberries every few days – do not remove them when still partially green or white – ripening produces natural sugars.

For delicate flowers, variegated foliage and sweet edible fruits, try planting a strawberry basket.

Country Cottage Windowbox

Windowboxes are particularly evocative of a rural idyll. For many of us, a cottage with roses around the door will remain a dream, but windowboxes of fragrant lavender, stocks and chamomile are perfectly achievable.

A terracotta trough can be suitably aged by painting it with natural yoghurt at the beginning of the season and then allowing nature's micro-organisms to do their work and break down the yoghurt to create an interesting 'look'.

Snow in summer and creeping jenny are plants known to many gardeners but are not often used in windowboxes and hanging baskets – their rampaging character will be contained by the box and they are both fairly hardy, although they will not stand drying out. Mimulus deserves a gold star for its longstanding versatility – flowering from late spring onwards, it produces rewarding blooms and trails prettily.

YOU WILL NEED

a terracotta trough
broken crocks or pebbles
multi-purpose potting compost
3 stocks (*Matthiola*) · 1 snow in
summer (*Cerastium*) · 1 dwarf
lavender (*Lavandula*
'Hidcote') · 1 Swedish ivy
(*Nepeta variegata*) · 1 cream
monkey flower (*Mimulus*)
1 creeping jenny (*Lysimachia
nummularia aurea*)
1 chamomile (*Anthemis*)

1 Check that your windowbox has drainage holes. Then cover these with a layer of crocks or pebbles. Add potting compost until it is level with the top of the box. Plan to have trailing plants to the fore and taller plants to the rear.

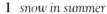

2 Space the stocks out. Make sure the crown of the root is 2–3 cm (1 in) below the surface. Add lavender and chamomile between the stocks, then, along the front, snow in summer, creeping jenny, Swedish ivy and mimulus.

QUICK TIPS

• Choose dwarf varieties of lavender or it will grow too tall and block the light.
• Deadhead stocks and they will bloom again.
• Age a terracotta windowbox by painting it with natural yoghurt and leaving it on the ground outside for a few weeks.
• Choose more unusual trailing plants, such as mimulus and campanula, for a country look.

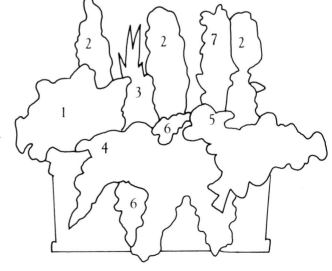

1 snow in summer
2 stocks
3 dwarf lavender
4 Swedish ivy
5 monkey flower
6 creeping jenny
7 chamomile

Use scented stocks, dwarf lavender and chamomile for a traditional combination of pastel colours.

Wildflower Windowbox

A windowbox of wildflowers makes an unusual contrast to bold displays of well-known plants. These European wildflowers are suitable for baskets and boxes.

Flowering from late spring to mid-summer
Yellow: rock rose, birdsfoot trefoil, horseshoe vetch, silverweed, monkey flower, feverfew
Blue: ivy-leaved toadflax, cornflower, heartsease, meadow cranesbill, bellflowers, wild thyme, wild marjoram
Pink/Red: herb Robert, pheasant's eye, poppy, mallow, dusky cranesbill, columbine
White: barren strawberry
Flowering from late summer to mid-autumn
Yellow: toadflax, creeping jenny, orange hawkweed
Blue: small scabious, bellflower, harebell
Flowering from late autumn to mid-spring
Yellow: primrose, cowslip, tormentil
White: wild strawberry, sweet woodruff
Blue: heartsease, germander speedwell, forget-me-not, dog violet
Pink: scarlet pimpernel, herb Robert

YOU WILL NEED

water-retaining pellets or gel
1 columbine (*Aquilegia vulgaris*)
1 cornflower (*Centaura*)
1 dwarf mallow (*Malva*)
1 feverfew
(*Tanacetum parthenium*)
1 oriental poppy (*Papaver*)
1 spotted dead nettle (*Lamium maculatum*)

1 Ensure that the box has drainage holes, then cover the base with crocks or pebbles. Fill loosely with multi-purpose compost, adding fertiliser granules halfway. Water-retaining pellets are a good idea as many wildflowers thrive in damp conditions.

2 Start by planting the taller columbine to one end, with the cornflower at the other. Infill with the mallow, feverfew and poppy, allowing the flowering deadnettle to spill over the front of the box. Top up with compost and water in well.

QUICK TIPS

• Wildflowers often thrive in semi-shady spots.
• Keep the compost moist; moisture-retaining gel is available and should be added when filling with compost.
• Provide adequate drainage by putting broken crocks or pebbles in the base.
• An asymmetrical arrangement can look particularly attractive. Plan your scheme to have larger plants at one end with perhaps a trailing plant at the other.
• Some garden centres have special wildflower areas – most plants are now clearly labelled but it is worth making enquiries if you need to check the compatibility of certain plants.

1 columbine
2 cornflower
3 dwarf mallow
4 feverfew
5 poppy
6 spotted deadnettle

Create an asymmetrical arrangement using graceful columbine, dwarf mallow, feverfew and deadnettle.

Wildflower Hanging Basket

A wildflower garden need not necessarily be a rambling meadow. A wildflower basket can provide you with sturdy flowers you recognise from the hedgerows of your childhood, with delicate blooms and fascinating foliage, all to be enjoyed as a compact sphere.

The one thing that could be a drawback with wildflowers is their brief flowering season but this can be overcome by planting chronologically so that at any one time some flowers are in bud while other blooms are fading. On page 60 we have listed wildflowers suitable for baskets and windowboxes and the seasons when they are in flower.

Your local garden centre is likely to have a wildflower section and you should be able to order other varieties through them. You should *never* take plants from the wild!

YOU WILL NEED

a 34-cm (14 in) wire
basket · moss
lightweight potting compost
a pot or bucket as a basket
holder
1 bellflower (*Campanula*)
1 pink wild geranium (dusky
cranesbill) (*Geranium*) · 1 blue
wild geranium (*Geranium*
'Johnson's Blue')
2 periwinkles (*Vinca*), one
variegated · 1 rock soapwort
(*Saponaria*) · 3 rock roses
(*Helianthemum*)

1 Having balanced the basket on a pot or bucket, start by lining the basket with damp moss, greener side outermost. Place a liner of plastic, foam or fibre in the base, then fill with compost, adding slow-release fertiliser granules halfway.

2 Plant the cranesbill and rock roses in the centre with the other plants at the sides. Guide these beneath the top wire to encourage them to trail down the sides and cover the base of the basket. Fill the basket with compost and water well.

QUICK TIPS
• Find the wildflower corner of your local garden centre and study the plant labels.
• A wildflower leaflet is sometimes available too.
• Choose flowers which bloom in the same season where possible.
• Plan your colour scheme in advance or opt for a random assortment as here.
• Keep the basket well watered and do not allow the compost to dry out.
• Never take plants from the wild.
• Thread some plants through the sides and base for a random ball arrangement.

1 *bellflower*
2 *wild geranium*
3 *periwinkle*
4 *rock soapwort*
5 *rock roses*

Recreate the beauty of the countryside with a random mix of red and yellow rock roses, blue geraniums and periwinkle.

A Scented Windowbox

Many plants with scented leaves need to be brushed past to release their perfume but those with blooms often release their scent in the cool of the evening.

The tobacco plants used here will flower in sun or partial shade and produce blooms from mid-summer until the early autumn frosts. These varieties can grow up to 30 cm (1 ft) tall which is quite tall enough for a windowbox but they also tend to lean forward and trail prettily. Some varieties of tobacco plant grow even taller – so do check when buying.

The dwarf lavender prefers a sunny position as does the scented pelargonium. These need to be planted in front of the tall tobacco plants where their foliage and scent will mingle.

One scented plant not used here is the lily. Dwarf varieties are now available.

Some windowboxes, such as this one, are fixed to the wall and will need to be planted in situ. Others have a plastic liner, which means that you can plant on a suitable surface and then slide the liner into the windowbox.

1 Check that your windowbox has drainage holes. You may need to drill some then line the box with slit plastic and crocks for drainage. Fill with a multi-purpose compost and plan your planting scheme before you plant up the box.

2 At this stage you could scatter some slow-release fertiliser about halfway down the box. Plant the large scented pelargonium so that it will trail over the front of the box. Then infill with the lavender and plant the taller tobacco plants to the rear.

QUICK TIPS

- Choose dwarf varieties of lavender and tobacco plants as some are fairly tall.
- Check that the tobacco plants you have chosen are fragrant – some varieties are more heavily scented than others.
- You can buy liners for wall-mounted windowboxes which make planting up far easier.
- Place your box where it will be brushed by people passing by, otherwise the scent will be released in only small quantities.
- Lavender and scented pelargoniums prefer a sunny site.

1 *white tobacco plants*
2 *mixed tobacco plants*
3 *lavender*
4 *lemon-scented pelargonium*

Combine colour and fragrance with red and white tobacco plants, dwarf lavender and lemon-scented pelargonium.

65

A Scented Basket

Hang a scented basket where you will brush against the leaves as you walk by, releasing their fragrance. Most helichrysum have no scent but this tiny-leaved version releases a wonderful aroma when you rub it between your fingers. Hanging baskets of this silvery plant alone can look most effective.

Pineapple mint, like all mint, can be invasive when planted in a container but it is worth including for its pleasant fruity fragrance when the leaves are gently crushed – hence its name. To make sure the mint does not spread too far, you can contain root growth by pushing in vertical sections of slate when planting, or simply keeping it in its pot.

Pinks (*Dianthus*) and heliotrope look good together and have a delicate perfume. The pansies are included not for their scent but to complement the colour scheme.

Pinks grow happily on poor soils and dislike soil that is rich or very acidic. If you have very chalky garden soil, you could mix a little of this, or slaked garden lime, into multi-purpose compost.

YOU WILL NEED

1 tray of pinks (8 *Dianthus* × *allwoodii* 'Doris') · 1 pineapple mint (*Mentha*) · 1 *Helichrysum microphylla* · 1 heliotrope 1 pot white pansies (*Viola hederacea*) · plastic for lining · hand-operated or electric drill · multi-purpose compost · wood preservative

1 If your basket is wooden, you will need to drill holes in the base first. Wood preservative will prevent it from rotting. Leave it to dry for a day then line it with slit plastic. Cover the base with pebbles and fill with mixed compost.

2 Start by planting the pinks centrally within the basket. Then add the heliotrope, helichrysum, pineapple mint and pansies in each of the four corners. Top up with compost then water in. Hang in a sunny position and deadhead regularly.

QUICK TIPS

● Prepare a wooden basket by drilling holes for drainage.
● Use a wood preservative to prolong the life of your basket.
● Line it with plastic to protect the timber.
● Cut slits for drainage.
● Pinks need full sun in order to flower so you may need to move your basket to a sunny spot.
● Helichrysum needs to be kept moist so daily watering is important.

● Stop the mint from spreading by keeping it within its pot or cornering it with slates.
● Add slaked lime to multi-purpose compost for pinks which dislike an acid soil.

1 *pinks*
2 *pineapple mint*
3 *heliotrope*
4 *helichrysum*
5 *pansies*

Pinks and heliotrope, offset by pineapple mint and helichrysum, will give a soft pastel scheme with a lingering fragrance.

A Windowbox for a Shady Area

Bring light into a shady spot with a windowbox of flowers and foliage.

Few of us would plan a windowbox for shade without being prompted but it can be particularly rewarding. You may not have a box overflowing with flowers but many shade-loving plants have graceful lines, strong colours and textures that work well together.

Some plants do flower in shade, of course. You could use busy lizzies or fuchsias. We chose to use bedding begonias, which flower in partial shade, for their lustrous dark leaves. The hardy deadnettle is also surprisingly attractive and can be found with yellow or pink blossoms.

Shade-loving plants appreciate moist conditions so it is worth including moisture-retaining gel when planting up.

1 Treat wooden boxes with wood preservative and allow to air for a day. Check that there are drainage holes and drill some if there are not. Line the base with crocks or pebbles and fill to halfway up the box with multi-purpose compost.

2 Add water-retaining pellets and slow-release fertiliser granules at the halfway stage. While they are still in their pots, plan how your plants are to look; i.e. where you would like trailing foliage, height and colour. Move them about until you are happy.

3 Start with the largest plant – in this case the fern – then plant the deadnettle at the other end of the box. Infill with hostas and begonias, with fuchsia trailing over the front.
Tip: snip off browning fronds or leaves.

YOU WILL NEED
—

a wooden windowbox 60 cm
(2 ft) long
wood preservative · plastic or
other liner · crocks or pebbles
multi-purpose compost
water-retaining gel
1 nephrolepis or Boston fern
(*Nephrolepis exaltata*
‘Bostoniensis’) · 2 hostas
(*H. fortunei* ‘Aureamarginata’)
1 yellow deadnettle (*Lamium
galeobdolon* ‘Herman’s
Pride’) · 1 *Fuchsia*
‘Autumnale’ · 3 bedding
begonia (*Begonia semperflorens*)

1 *Boston fern*
2 *hosta*
3 *deadnettle*
4 Fuchsia ‘*Autumnale*’
5 *bedding begonia*

Textured ferns and variegated cream and green hostas contrast well with bright begonias in a coral container.

A Hanging Basket for a Shady Spot

Shady corners should not be forgotten. Warm planting schemes like these shades of peach are quite in order.

The sunny border in your garden is frequently the most colourful and the shadiest spot often a problem area. Most hanging baskets thrive in sun but many plants also bloom well in semi-shade.

Fuchsias, in particular, are known for their partiality to shade and busy lizzies, too, will flower without sunshine as long as they are placed in the shade only after the first flowers have opened.

Some gardeners are surprised to learn that begonias will flower in partial shade. Pansies are known as winter-flowering plants so it is not unusual for them to bloom in a shady corner.

The alternative is to choose plants that have particularly attractive foliage – ferns and hostas are an obvious choice. These need damp soil and moist conditions, so frequent spraying and a water-retaining agent are important.

1 Gather your ingredients. Place the basket on a bucket to prevent it from rocking, then line it with damp moss, green side outermost. Line it with plastic, then fill it with compost, including water-retaining and slow-release fertiliser granules.

2 Plant the fuchsia, busy lizzie and monkey flower on three sides of the basket with the upright begonia in the centre. Arrange the convolvulus to trail beneath the top wire. Plant one of the busy lizzies through the sides. Then water in well.

QUICK TIPS

● Avoid splashing water on the leaves of the begonia as this can cause rotting.
● Shade-loving plants generally appreciate lots of water, so keep the compost moist. Fuchsias and begonias both need plenty of water.

● Take a closer look at the strongly defined foliage plants, including most ferns. They can look surprisingly attractive, particularly if your windowbox is painted a bold colour.
● Many winter-flowering plants, such as pansies, will flower in shady spots.

YOU WILL NEED

a 36-cm (14 in) basket · moss
multi-purpose compost
plastic or other liner
1 coral begonia (*Begonia*
'Chanson')
1 *Convolvulus mauritanicus*
1 semi-trailing fuchsia
(*F.* 'Orange Crystal')
1 monkey flower (*Mimulus*)
2 busy lizzies

1 *coral begonia*
2 *convolvulus*
3 *semi-trailing fuchsia*
4 *monkey flower*
5 *busy lizzie*

Choose deep peach and blues for an unusual colour combination of flowers for a shady spot.

An Alpine Windowbox

The small size and delicate appearance of alpines often belies their hardiness. Used to surviving in mountainous regions, they can withstand dry periods but dislike being overwatered.

You will need a mix of fine horticultural grit and compost to provide a well-drained soil. A thick layer of gravel or crocks on the base of the box is also important. Terracotta is a particularly suitable material for an alpine windowbox as any excess moisture will drain away naturally through the porous walls and base of the box. (You will still need drainage holes, of course.) Plan your scheme by placing the plants in their pots within the windowbox. Aim to mix flowering and foliage plants and to group complementary colours together.

You may well feel tempted by other alpines when faced with a display at your garden centre or nursery. Whatever you choose, it is worth including the alpine favourites: sedums and saxifrage, houseleeks, lewisia and rock roses.

YOU WILL NEED

fine horticultural grit
multi-purpose compost
creeping jenny
(*Lysimachia nummularia*)
thrift (*Armeria maritima*
'Dusseldorf Pride')
houseleek (*Sempervivum*
'Wolcott')
Campanula carpatica
1 *Chrysanthemum hosmariense*
1 *Silene schafta* 'Robusta'

1 Start by mixing the grit and compost in roughly 50/50 proportions. Then line the base of the windowbox with a substantial layer of broken pot crocks or pebbles. The rooting system of alpines is very shallow so they will not need deep compost.

2 Tap, rather than twist, the plants from their pots, then gently tease out the root system before planting. Starting at one end, work along the box, planting one plant to the front and the next to the rear; a large stone in the middle looks effective.

3 Water in carefully, avoiding the crowns of the plants and the tops of leaves as alpines do not like to be waterlogged. If there are spaces to fill, you can add other suitable plants later on. Look in the alpine section of your garden centre.

1 creeping jenny
2 thrift
3 houseleek
4 campanula
5 chrysanthemum
6 silene

Make the most of delicate alpine flowers with an eye-level container. Pink thrift and blue dwarf bellflower will spread and intermingle.

An Alpine Hanging Basket

Alpines prefer a sunny situation and dryish soil, so water sparingly. If you have a particularly rainy week, it is worth sheltering the plants under cover for a while. Alpines hate having wet roots so you must make sure that the drainage is good. Mix the compost half and half with horticultural grit to give a free-draining mixture. We used a thin fibre liner through which moisture can pass. It has slits to enable planting at lower levels so that plants can cover the base of the basket.

This basket was planted in early spring when most of the plants were very small and relatively inexpensive. It is composed of plants which will flower in groups from early spring to late summer and early autumn. Hung eventually from a post of climbing clematis, it creates an exceptionally pretty corner beside a doorway.

YOU WILL NEED

fine horticultural grit
multi-purpose compost
3 *Gypsophila repens* 'Dubia'
1 *Veronica pectinata*
1 tumbling ted (*Saponaria ocymoides*)
1 *Campanula* 'Birch Hybrid'
3 *Geranium sanguineum striatum*
1 *Sedum spurium* 'Album'
1 *Sedum spurium* 'Purple Carpet'
1 *Diascia* 'Ruby Field'
1 *Sisyrinchium* 'Mrs Spivey'
1 pink (*Dianthus* 'Dewdrop')
1 rock rose
(*Helianthemum* 'The Bride')

1 Gather your ingredients. Plan to have trailing plants at the sides and the more upright sisyrinchium, rock rose and pink in the centre. Begin by inserting the liner and mixture of grit and compost. Then plant the rock rose and pink.

2 Plant the geraniums and gypsophila in clumps to form larger plants later. Encircle the pink with trailing plants, planting from below and through the slits in the liner wherever possible. Water in gently and place in a sunny spot.

QUICK TIPS

● Alpines like well-drained soil so mix half horticultural grit and half multi-purpose compost in a bucket before starting to fill your basket.
● Many alpines dislike having the top of their root ball (the crown) watered. Aim to water in between plants where possible.
● Make slits in fibre liners for planting through the sides and base to ensure an evenly covered hanging basket.
● Choose plants that flower in succession whenever possible.

1 Gypsophila repens
2 *veronica*
3 *tumbling ted*
4 *campanula*
5 *geranium*
6 *sedum*
7 *diascia*
8 *sisyrinchium*
9 *pink*
10 *rock rose*

For alpine flowers all year round, this combination includes gypsophila, pinks, tumbling ted and sedums.

AUTUMN PLANTS

All too often, as mid-autumn approaches and our bright summer baskets die off, gardeners empty their hanging baskets and windowboxes and put them away until the following spring.

The autumn and winter months are just the time when your house and garden need extra life and colour and this can be very easily achieved simply by clearing dead foliage and adding in hardier plants which can withstand colder, less sunny conditions and still give a good display of gentle colour and texture.

Autumn Windowbox

Instead of the usual gold and yellow colours of autumn which, incidentally, can be achieved with a mix of miniature chrysanthemums, we have opted for a more delicate silver grey and pink scheme. Planted in mid-autumn, it will still be looking healthy in early spring, by which time the plants will have intermingled charmingly.

YOU WILL NEED

a stone or similar windowbox (terracotta would clash with the pink shades)
1 *Hebe* 'Seduisante' (purple)
1 *Hebe* 'Kirkii' (white-flowering)
1 *Artemisia* 'Powys Castle' (scented)
3 pink/white heathers
4 ornamental cabbages (2 each of pink and white)

1 After ensuring that there are drainage holes, line the base of the box with broken crocks or pebbles. Half-fill the windowbox with ericaceous (acidic) soil. Test your planting plan. Aim to have larger plants to the rear.

2 Hebes grow fairly tall – up to 75 cm (30 in). Once you are happy with your plan, firm the largest plants in first. Then infill with the heathers and ornamental cabbage along the front, alternating pink and white as we have done in our arrangement.

QUICK TIPS

● Use ericaceous (lime-free) compost for hebes and heathers – you can buy this ready prepared in bags, or mix your own using multi-purpose potting compost and a powder.
● Only use hebes if you have a fairly tall window.

Windowboxes can be used to give you extra privacy if the planting arrangement is tall.
● Heathers like a rich, moist compost so keep the arrangement well watered and this windowbox will survive for years.

1 Hebe 'Kirkii'
2 Hebe 'Seduisante'
3 artemisia
4 heathers
5 ornamental cabbage

For an autumn scheme of pink, white and silver grey, opt for hebes and heathers infilled with ornamental cabbages.

AUTUMN HANGING BASKET

A Pansy Ball

One of the most reliable flowers for autumn and winter baskets has to be the pansy but rather than the usual half hanging basket, you could try a pansy ball.

It is possible to wire together two standard half-baskets or you can now buy basket balls which clip together. If making your own, try to choose smaller baskets as, once filled with soil and water, they are very heavy indeed.

You can buy a tray of plug plants in mid-spring. These are easy to insert from the outside. If using a wire basket, you will need to line it with moss and polythene.

To make planting easier, you could balance each half on a filled flowerpot.

Allow the baskets to settle for a few days before joining, or overfill one half. Otherwise there will be insufficient compost and moisture around the plants in the top section of the ball.

YOU WILL NEED
---
tray of 48 plug pansies (*Viola* 'Padparadja Forerunner Tangerine')
moss-polythene liner
multi-purpose potting compost
2 hanging baskets, 36 cm (14 in) in diameter

1 Start by making holes at regular intervals around the base of the first half. Insert the plugs from the outside, roots first. Wrap the roots in a small cone of polythene to prevent them from being damaged. Add layers of compost as you work upwards.

2 Before joining, water in to allow the compost to settle. Overfill one half of the basket and cover it with plastic. Invert it over the second basket and slide the plastic out. If it is not a clip-together version, wire the two halves together.

QUICK TIPS
- Overfill both baskets so that, when placed together, the compost is compact and there are no airpockets where plant roots could dry out.
- Wrap plant roots in a cone of plastic (rather than damp newspaper) as this will slide through more easily.
- A small, empty flowerpot buried in the top half will make watering easier. If this pot will be visible when the ball is hung up, you can drop in a potted-up pansy and then simply remove it for watering.

- If you have a plastic, clip-together ball, you can plant a pansy ball later in the season, using full-size plants. To make the gaps large enough to insert the pansy root from the outside in, clip away the vertical or horizontal plastic struts.
  To maintain the strength of the ball, ensure that these enlarged gaps are not made directly beside each other.
- Remove the chains while infilling with pansies but remember their positions while planting up.

A ball of autumn pansies of this unusual orange-red variety will bring colour through the winter months.

EVERGREEN PLANTS

Although many of us opt for evergreens such as ivy somewhere in our spring and summer baskets, it is rare to see an evergreen basket bringing life to a doorway through the winter months. However, the bright-berried plants and tiny flowered evergreens, with their glossy and red or gold-tinged foliage, will last through some of the coldest weather and can bring a great deal of pleasure.

Most evergreens are far hardier than summer bedding plants and are unlikely to suffer the problems of drying out through the damp winter months as watering once a week or so will be sufficient unless the weather is particularly mild and windy.

An Evergreen Hanging Basket

Evergreens merit greater use than only in winter or as backdrop foliage; they are also extremely useful in baskets hung in shady spots – box, elaeagnus, periwinkle, creeping fig and ferns are all successful in deep or semi-shade.

YOU WILL NEED

moss · plastic liner
multi-purpose compost
1 *Cotoneaster salicifolius*
'Autumn Fire'
1 *Cotoneaster dammeri*
1 periwinkle (*Vinca major
variegata*)

1 Collect your ingredients. You will need moss and a plastic liner to help to hold water. Some slits in the plastic will be necessary for drainage. Remove the chains, if possible, to make planting easier. Line the basket with moss, greener side outermost.

2 Add the plastic liner, fill with compost. Set the upright cotoneaster to the rear and the periwinkle trailing over and through the sides. Add compost and water well. Replace the chains, and hang from a strong bracket. Feed after a few months.

QUICK TIPS

● Use versatile evergreens as a foliage backdrop to year-round planting, for winter schemes and in shady spots.
● Water weekly. If evergreen plants in a hanging basket appear to be drying out, immerse in a bucket of water until bubbles stop rising. The root ball is now moist. Rehang and water every few weeks throughout the winter months.

● Aim to cover the base of the basket by encouraging plants to trail through the sides.
● Terracotta and glazed ceramic containers can crack in winter – so you may need to move them in hard frosts. Some, of course, are frost-proof.

1 Cotoneaster salicifolius
2 Cotoneaster dammeri
3 *periwinkle*

The glossy leaves and red berries of cotoneaster intermingle with variegated periwinkle in a midwinter basket.

An Evergreen Windowbox

At a time when most garden plants have died back and lost their colour and leaves you can still bring cheer to the dull winter months with lustrous skimmias, red-tinged leucothoe and feathery juniper.

Leaf colour and texture are part of the joy of winter gardening, although evergreen plants will give colour and strength to a display all year round. Once winter is over, you can add spring and summer flowers to contrast with the glossy foliage.

You might think these shrubs would grow too large for windowboxes and hanging baskets but all plants adapt their size to suit the container they live in and are restrained in their growth and spread by the size of their root ball.

The glossy green leaves and purple sprouting of the skimmia will look good beside the colourful red leaves of the leucothoe. The spreading juniper gives contrasting shape and texture to the arrangement.

1 First plan your arrangement with the plants still in their pots. Consider the shape of the spreading fir and the situation of your windowbox in relation to shrubs below or climbers growing around your window.

2 It is often safer to plant boxes in situ or to fill a plastic liner. Having half-filled your box with multi-purpose compost, infill with the largest plants first and finally the berried gaultheria. Finally, add compost to just below the top edge of the box.

QUICK TIPS
- Choose a group of plants with foliage that is varied in both colour and texture.
- Plan for one plant to trail over and break the line of the box.
- With heavy stone or composite boxes, either plant in situ or fill a plastic liner separately then slot it in.
- Larger plants will be restrained by the space allowed to the root ball and so will not grow excessively large.

YOU WILL NEED

plastic liner for the box
multi-purpose compost
2 *Skimmia japonica* 'Rubella'
1 *Juniperus sabina*
'Tamariscifolia' (spreading fir)
1 *Leucothoe axillaris* 'Scarletta'
1 *Gaultheria procumbens*
(berried)

1 Skimmia japonica
2 *juniper*
3 *leucothoe*
4 *gaultheria*

Accentuate the glowing foliage of leucothoe by mixing it with the glossy leaves of skimmias and gaultheria and feathery fronds of juniper.   83

CHRISTMAS FOLIAGE

From the gold-tinged leaves of variegated holly to the luminous white of cyclamen and glossy, berried evergreens, Christmas offers an opportunity for some delightful schemes.

A Christmas Hanging Basket

You may never have thought of making a hanging basket specifically for the Christmas season but among all the artificial tinsel and glitz it will seem refreshingly delicate and natural.

Roses can last for two weeks or longer if provided with phials of water of the type usually provided for orchids. These can be wired and hidden among the greenery.

Red ribbons make decorative hangings and the cyclamen will survive happily in a sheltered porch while temperatures are at freezing or just above.

YOU WILL NEED

multi-purpose compost/plastic
woven twig basket and wreath
34 cm (13 in) in diameter
wide red/gold, wired ribbon
1 m (3 ft) long, 6 cm (2½ in)
red ribbon
3 m (10 ft), 2.5 cm (1 in) wide
8 plastic phials
1 cyclamen · 8 white roses
4 small ivies (*Hedera*)
1 stem of eucalyptus,
snowberries (*Symphoricarpos*)

1 Collect the ingredients. Line the basket with slit plastic and start by filling it with the cyclamen sitting upright in the centre and the ivies trailing over the sides. Top up with lightweight multi-purpose compost. Water carefully.

2 Cut the rose stems to 20 cm (8 in) and thread them through the wreath into phials of water. Thread the larger green stems around the wreath first, finishing with the more delicate ruscus and snowberries and also inserting these into the phials.

QUICK TIPS
● Small plastic phials of the type available from florists, and generally used for orchids and corsages, will give an arrangement such as this a lifespan of around two weeks.
● If a frost is forecast, bring the arrangement into a cool hallway for the night.
● Use wire-edged ribbon for impressive bows – it is easier to tie and far less floppy.
● If you wish for a more permanent Christmas basket without phials of water, simply combine cyclamen and ivy in a container and hang it up on red ribbons.

1 roses
2 cyclamen
3 eucalyptus
4 snowberry
5 ivy

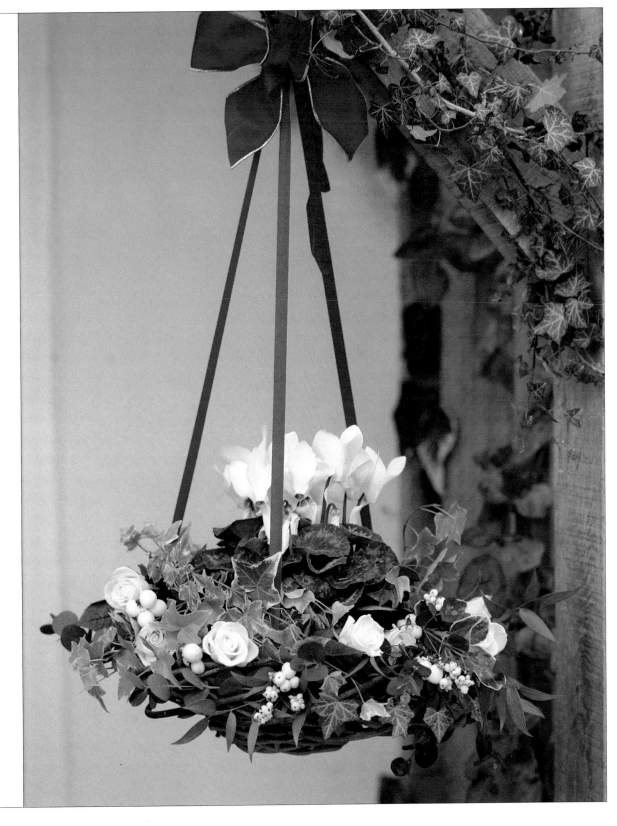

Tie the narrow ribbons on to the outer wicker wreath to form a balanced arrangement when held from the top and tie the wreath to a cup-hook, or something similar, secured into a timber porch frame. Tie the wired ribbon into a large bow and pin it on to hide the top fastenings.

A festive red and white combination of roses and cyclamen wound about a rustic wreath with ivy and snowberries.

A Christmas Windowbox with a Tree

Add to the seasonal festivities with a tree-filled windowbox full of Christmas charm.

Dramatic red berries, glossy green leaves and symmetrical fir trees, enhanced by the mellow warmth of a teak window box, make a Christmas arrangement that is both traditional and yet satisfyingly unfamiliar so that it will catch the attention of visitors and friends.

For too many of us, outside Christmas decorations are limited to fairy lights and a door wreath when, in fact, there is a wealth of plants in the garden centre with leaves that have an interesting shape or texture or bear bright berries, just waiting to be grouped in seasonal harmony.

This arrangement will last from mid-autumn until spring with little care needed, apart from a weekly watering. If you wish, you could add various extra decorations, such as silver or gold chains of stars, for the Christmas week but this balance of Christmas colour has a subtle charm of its own that really needs no extra adornment.

YOU WILL NEED

plastic liner for box
ericaceous compost
2 *Skimmia reevesiana*
3 ivies (*Hedera*)
4 small upright conifers

1 Gather together your ingredients. Start by making holes in the plastic liner of the box, then add a small layer of grit or crocks to aid drainage. Half-fill the box with ericaceous compost (for acid-loving plants) to maintain healthy growth.

2 Firm in the two largest plants (the skimmias) leaning their berried leaves towards the front where possible. Follow this by planting the four upright conifers to the rear. Infill at each end and along the front with the ivies to soften the edges.

QUICK TIPS

● Use berried plants other than holly in Christmas baskets to create an arrangement that is slightly unusual.

● Water weekly once the Christmas period is over and this windowbox is likely to last for at least a year or even longer.

● Despite being hardwood, teak windowboxes benefit from a treatment of wood preservative to keep them looking warm and mellow. An alternative is to use a plastic liner.

1 *skimmia*
2 *ivy*
3 *conifers*

Four miniature conifers and glossy-berried skimmias create a refreshingly natural display for Christmas.

A Christmas Trug as an Indoor Arrangement

For a more unusual Christmas colour scheme, we decided to opt for gold and green, bringing indoors plants that are often banished to the garden.

This arrangement could be used on a deep windowsill or even in a large fireplace if watered regularly. The plants could be moved to the garden after Christmas if you wish. A few days before you plant up the trug, stain it in your chosen colour. We decided on spruce green in order not to detract from the colour scheme and yet still be in keeping with a Christmas theme. Leave it to dry thoroughly for a few days, then line it with plastic. If you make drainage holes, you will need to water the trug outside, otherwise careful watering is essential in order to avoid waterlogging.

YOU WILL NEED

ericaceous potting compost
a large garden trug
dark green woodstain
large candle · narrow gold
ribbon
1 m (3 ft) gold cord
a gold cherub and 3 gold baubles
florist's wire · 5 dried quince
osmanthus (*Osmanthus heterophyllus* 'Tricolour')
yellow fir (*Thuja orientalis*)
spotted laurel (*Aucuba japonica*)
Euonymus fortunei
Euphorbia · 4 ivies

1 Half-fill the trug with a lightweight ericaceous compost as the osmanthus, in particular, is an acid-loving plant. Start by firming in the largest plants (the *Thuja* and spotted laurel), twisting the pots gently to remove the rootball intact.

2 Bear in mind where the trug will sit so that you can position smaller plants to the front. Once the larger plants are in, you can wind the narrow gold ribbon around the candle and choose a place for it where its flame cannot burn the trug handle.

3 Place the candle firmly in position so that it cannot fall over. Add the smaller ivy and, once the trug is in place, arrange the quince both inside and out. Finally, wind the thicker gold cord around the handle and wire on the cherub and baubles.

1 osmanthus
2 Thuja orientalis
3 euonymus
4 ivy
5 spotted laurel
6 euphorbia
7 quince

The harmonious tones of thuja and holly combine with spotted laurel and shiny baubles to make a basket of rich greens and golds.

CHILDREN'S BASKETS AND BOXES

It is not always possible to find a suitable space for your children to garden nor to keep a child's garden contained within a set area. This is where baskets and windowboxes prove rewarding.

Choose bright colours and easy-to-grow plants that are not likely to disappoint. Petunias and marigolds are an obvious choice, as are busy lizzies and lobelia.

Results from windowboxes and hanging baskets are relatively speedy. Rather than growing from seed, use plants of a reasonable size so that growing time is reasonably short.

A Hanging Basket for Children

Children will enjoy planting up baskets. To them, daily watering is not a chore but a pleasure, although you will have to check that watering is carried out regularly and not overenthusiastically! A simple basket could be the start of an interest in gardening for years to come.

YOU WILL NEED

a wire basket
moss · plastic liner
multi-purpose potting compost
2 *Petunia* 'Red Stripe'
6 busy lizzies
2 *Verbena* 'Red Cascade'
1 helichrysum

1 Let the children line the basket with moss, greener side outermost. Line it with slit plastic. Half-fill the basket with compost and plant the petunias in the top. An attractive alternative would be a trailing petunia hybrid.

2 With some adult help, plant the busy lizzies at intervals through the sides of the basket so that they will eventually almost cover the base. The verbena and helichrysum can be planted below the top line of the basket so that they will trail.

3 After planting, top up with compost and water in well. It is worth allowing the children the responsibility of daily watering and deadheading blooms so that they can appreciate the results of their first attempt and may try other arrangements.

1 *petunia*
2 *busy lizzie*
3 *verbena*
4 *helichrysum*

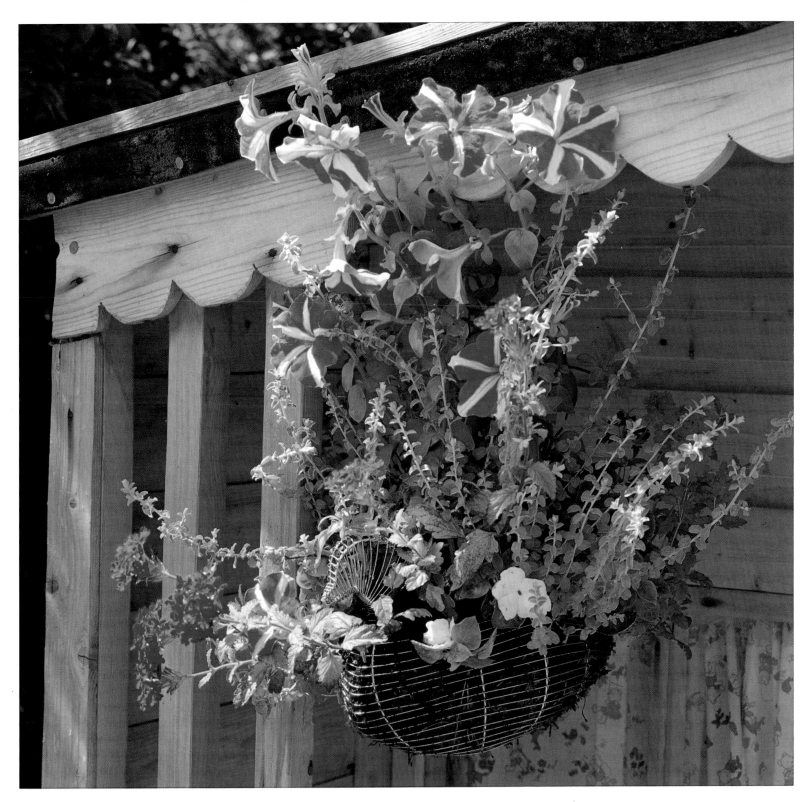

Red-and-white-striped petunias, cascading verbena and white busy lizzies will meet most children's desire for bright simplicity.

Children's Windowboxes

Yellow marigolds and orange nasturtiums seem made for children as they are easy-to-grow summer annuals that make a splash of colour.

Children like to be part of every stage in gardening, from selecting plants (you will need to guide them towards compact, bushy plants) to planting and watering.

If you discuss the heights to which the plants will grow, the children will see the logic of planting them in descending order, with the trailing plants at the front. This is the ideal opportunity for a botany lesson – how root systems work, how plants use chlorophyll to turn sunlight into food.

We used a number of plants in order to give an impressive display – many more and the amount of soil and water the basket can hold would not support them. Should you notice any pending disasters, you can do a little surreptitious gardening or replacement after the gardeners have gone to bed, to avoid unnecessary disappointment.

YOU WILL NEED

multi-purpose potting compost
slow-release fertiliser
water-retaining granules
2 Felicia amelloides
4 French marigolds (Tagetes patula)
3 lobelia
3 snapdragons (Antirrhinum)
1 golden marguerite (Anthemis)
2 nasturtiums (Tropaeolum)

---

1 Make drainage holes in the base of the windowbox if there are none. Add a few handfuls of gravel for drainage, then half-fill with multi-purpose compost and some slow-release fertiliser and water-retaining granules (optional).

2 Plant the golden marguerites and snapdragons to the rear, with the French marigolds and nasturtiums in the centre and lobelia at the front. Arrange the felicia to trail over one side. Top up with compost, firm in the plants and water well.

QUICK TIPS

• Allow the children to choose the colours of plants for themselves if possible. Bright colours are likely to be most popular.
• Choose fairly reliable plants, such as marigolds, lobelia and petunias, and aim to keep an eye on them yourself.
• Let the children plant the basket or windowbox and take care of it by watering and deadheading.
• Small baskets tend to dry out very quickly so are not a good idea.
• Be very careful that any plants you use are not poisonous.

1 golden marguerites
2 French marigolds
3 lobelia
4 snapdragons
5 felicia
6 nasturtiums

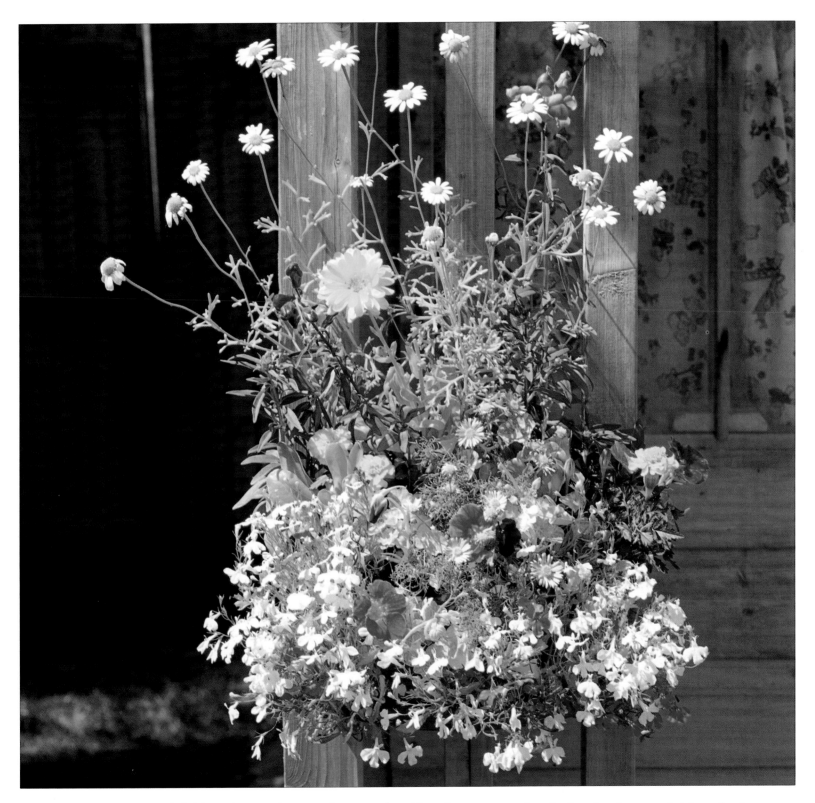

Choose the flowers of childhood – snapdragons, daisies, marigolds and nasturtiums for a basket that brims with life and colour.

93

BUDGET IDEAS:
A Budget Hanging Basket

It is easy to buy plants in season and create impressive windowboxes and baskets in the space of an hour but this can prove expensive. Many plants can be grown from seed or cuttings and others bought to infill, if necessary, when your basket or box is ready to be planted up.

Fuchsias, pelargoniums, *Petunia* 'Surfinia', and busy lizzie are all easy to grow from cuttings. You can simply stand the cutting in a glass of water for a couple of weeks until several white roots have grown. The more professional method, however, is to cut the stem straight across, dip it in hormone rooting powder and insert it in a seeding potting compost that is 50% sharp sand and 50% peat.

YOU WILL NEED

36-cm (14 in) basket
multi-purpose compost
slow-release fertiliser
foam liner
1 packet lobelia seed
1 packet *Bidens aurea* seed
6 busy lizzie
2 *Petunia* 'Surfinia'
2 *Fuchsia* 'Blowick'
2 *Verbena* 'Sissinghurst'

1 Sow the seed thinly in trays of fine potting compost in early spring. Water with a fine spray. Cover with cling film and keep in a warm place until the first leaves appear. Remove the cover. Prick out the seedlings at around 5 cm (2 in) tall.

2 The fuchsia, 'Surfinia' and busy lizzie can be grown from cuttings. We lined our basket with foam which is a good water retainer and can be hidden by plants. Plant the fuchsia in the centre, angling the other plants to trail through.

QUICK TIPS
● Use a saucer and knife to help to control the position of the seeds on the compost.
● Cover the seeds with cling film with holes pierced in it to prevent too much condensation. When the first leaves appear, lift the cling film each day to 'air' the plants.
● Leave the seed tray in a warm, light but not too bright place to allow the seeds to germinate. If it seems very bright, lay a sheet of newspaper over the tray.
● When pricking out, hold the seedlings by their top leaves not by the roots. Use a pencil to make holes in the compost.

1 *lobelia*
2 *busy lizzie*
3 *fuchsia*
4 Petunia 'Surfinia'
5 *verbena*
6 Bidens aurea

Create a basket brimming with colour from seeds and cuttings. Fuchsias, 'Surfinia', verbena and *Bidens aurea* are prolific.

A Budget Windowbox

You can achieve a spectacular windowbox with a very low financial outlay. Most of these plants were grown from cuttings and the trailing lobelia and verbena from seed. Growing from seed is easier if you have a greenhouse but seeds and cuttings will also grow happily on a warm windowsill.

Start the seeds off in a tray of moist compost placed in a warm place for ten days or so. Cover the tray with cling film with tiny holes in it. If necessary, use a sheet of newspaper to keep out very bright light. Ready-made windowbox gardening kits are now available with narrow seed boxes and raised, clear-plastic lids with air holes. Once the seeds have germinated and the first leaves appear, take off the cover and move the tray to a sunny position.

YOU WILL NEED

1 packet lobelia seeds
1 packet verbena seeds
1 packet white
daisy (*Bellis*) seeds
1 pendulous begonia
1 bedding begonia
5 busy lizzies (*Impatiens
walleriana*)
2 zonal pelargoniums
(*Pelargonium × hortorum*)
a seed tray
multi-purpose compost
crocks or gravel
season-long fertiliser
water-retaining granules
(optional)

1 Sow the lobelia and verbena in early spring, pricking out the seedlings a month later. Take cuttings of other plants before the first frosts arrive, planting them in pots after four weeks or so. Feed the compost weekly with liquid fertilizer.

2 Plant up your windowbox at the end of spring. Fill with a layer of crocks, then multi-purpose compost. Plant the pelargoniums, busy lizzies and begonias, then infill with trailing plants.

QUICK TIPS

- Mix tiny seeds with very dry sand to make fine planting easier.
- Cover germinating seeds with cling film to keep the compost moist or newspaper to keep out very bright light.
- Root cuttings in a mixture of 50% peat and 50% sharp sand.

- If seedlings start to become too leggy in their search for light, build up soil around the stem and move them somewhere a little cooler.
- Make a note of planting times and how your seeds progress, for reference in future years.

1 lobelia
2 verbena
3 pendulous begonia
4 bedding begonia
5 busy lizzies
6 pelargoniums
7 white daisies

A windowbox in shades of blue, pink and purple can cost very little when grown from seeds and cuttings.

How to Hang a Basket

Choosing a site

A spot that receives both sun and shade is best. Avoid north- and south-facing walls if possible, as these are often too shady or too hot. A draughty corner is also best avoided.

A number of plants will thrive in shady areas. Take a look at our schemes on pages 68–71. Shade-loving plants for summer include begonias, bellflowers, busy lizzie, creeping fig, ferns, fuchsia, honeysuckle, hosta, jasmine, monkey flower, pansy, philodendron, pick-a-back plant and tobacco plants.

In spring, bulbs such as lily of the valley, daffodils, tulips and snake's head fritillary will flower happily in semi-shade. Other spring-flowering plants which enjoy partially shaded sites include periwinkle, primrose, violets and azaleas.

Brackets

Wrought iron is the strongest and most suitable material. Choose a size to suit the diameter of your basket and to allow some space between your basket and the wall to prevent the basket from touching the wall and damaging the plants.

Basket size	Bracket size
26 cm (10 in)	23 cm (9 in)
30 cm (12 in)	23 cm (9 in)
36 cm (14 in)	23 cm (9 in)
41 cm (16 in)	30 cm (12 in)
46 cm (18 in)	30 cm (12 in)
51 cm (20 in)	36 cm (14 in)
61 cm (24 in)	41 cm (16 in)
76 cm (30 in)	46 cm (18 in)

The bracket will have to cope with a heavy load, so secure it properly with screws and fixing plugs of the correct gauge and length. Check for tightness from time to time throughout the year.

YOU WILL NEED

electric drill with correct size drill bit for screws
extension cable
screws – usually provided but otherwise 5 cm (2 in) long
wallplugs of the same length, standard or cavity depending on surface, i.e. brick or render
coloured crayon · measuring tape
straight or crosshead screwdriver

Practical tips

Fixing up a bracket is very similar to putting up a shelf bracket. Baskets are very heavy when full and being watered and will need sturdy fixings. Most brackets come with the correct length of screw and wallplug. If you are fixing into render, a cavity wallplug, which splays out when inserted, is a good choice.

First ensure that the surface your bracket will rest on is relatively smooth. The top screw will be taking most of the strain, so ensure that this will be secured into a solid surface, i.e. brick rather than mortar.

Imagine the height that your basket will fall to once hung by the chains. Do not make it too high as you do not want

right and far right: rise and fall device

wooden bracket with hook

standard wrought iron

Victorian-style wrought iron

to see only the underside of the basket. However, you also need to take into account whether it will be in the way of anyone walking by and if it is likely to be a danger. A heavy basket can cause an unpleasant accident if it is in an unexpected place.

It is most important to measure accurately as you do not wish to make more holes than necessary. The rule here is to measure twice and drill once! Mark the spots you intend to drill with coloured crayon.

Then, holding the drill at right angles to the wall, maintain a light pressure when drilling. Drill in approximately 3 cm (1½ in). (You can mark this measurement on your drill bit with tape or move the bit into the drill to the correct length.) Then insert the rawlplug and, holding the bracket in position, put in the screw. Leave tightening until both screws are in position.

When fixing into a wooden post or fence, carry out the same procedure but without wall plugs.

How to put up a Windowbox

Many windowboxes will sit securely on deep sills but as they are so heavy, it is still important to fasten them to the sill. If the box is wooden, you can use angle brackets at the front or sides, drilling and screwing these to secure the box. Otherwise, a length of decorative cast iron along the front of the sill makes an attractive safety option. Again mark first with a crayon and drill and screw the cast iron on, using wallplugs for a sturdy result.

Some sills slope and here you will

Fixing a windowbox

1 *Hang U-shaped brackets (bought to fit the windowbox) where there is no sill. Fix securely into the brickwork or render using wallplugs and screws of at least 5 cm (2 in) in length. Then screw the front of the windowbox to the brackets.*

2 *If the box is to sit on a sill, fix L-shaped brackets to the base of the sill with the fronts projecting upwards. Sit the box on the brackets and screw them on to the front of the box.*

---

need to place wedges beneath the box to ensure that it is level.

For windows that do not have sills, you can put up windowboxes underneath the window, secured by underneath brackets. Installation is much the same as when putting up shelves.

Begin by marking out in pencil where the box is to be fixed. Then, spacing the brackets evenly along the base, mark

---

where holes are to be drilled. Draw lines between the marks and check that they are in a straight line. Adjust where necessary. Drill holes using the correct size of bit for the screws. Place the brackets in position and insert the screws halfway. When all screws are in, tighten up evenly.

Small plastic windowboxes, such as those used for children's boxes, can rest on two screws secured into a fence or wall. Here, you are unlikely to require wall plugs.

Hanging Basket Liners

The first hanging baskets were made of twisted wire lined with sphagnum moss and filled with a peat-based or multi-purpose compost. For a large number of gardeners, this is still the preferred method as such baskets have a natural appearance, although today's wire baskets are usually plastic-coated.

Many gardeners now include a polythene liner with slits in it or a saucer to aid water retention. Various other devices also help to prevent waterlogging or drying out.

Foam, recycled 'whalehide' paper, fabric and coconut-fibre liners are available with overlapping flaps and can be cut to fit any size of basket. These are usually available as overlapping petals, and planting through the slits of these liners enables you to cover the base of the basket.

Rigid cardboard liners are made of a compressed paper substance that is bio-degradable but will not last more than one year. They hold water well but you cannot plant through the sides unless you punch holes in the liner.

Solid-plastic hanging baskets are becoming more popular, particularly those with a false base or reservoir for conserving water. This overcomes one of the greatest problems encountered with hanging baskets – infrequent watering. It is not possible to plant through the sides, however, unless there are ready-made holes, so the use of trailing plants to disguise large areas of plastic is important.

Drainage Materials

Some windowboxes, such as the more expensive teak varieties, come with plastic liners. It is worth coating all wooden windowboxes with a wood preservative before planting up. Most windowboxes planned for outdoor use, including those made of terracotta, plastic, stone and composites, will not require a liner but should have drainage

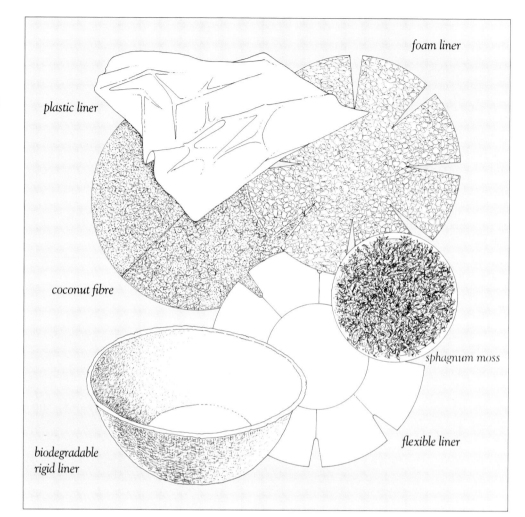

plastic liner

foam liner

coconut fibre

sphagnum moss

biodegradable rigid liner

flexible liner

holes drilled into the base if there are none already. These holes should be covered with a layer of crocks.

Crocks are broken-up terracotta pots which are used to cover the drainage holes in windowboxes. This prevents compost from being washed away. Large pebbles can also be used.

Some plants, such as herbs, alpines and bulbs, need a well-drained environment and will benefit from a layer of horticultural grit over the crocks. Grit is also mixed into the compost in the ratio 50:50 and used as a top layer around alpines to prevent them from rotting.

Compost

A peat-based mixture is mainly used for hanging baskets that will be supporting plants for only one season. Peat-based compost is lightweight, contains added nutrients and is particularly good at retaining water. The nutrients tend to be washed out by frequent watering but this can be countered by regular feeding.

A multi-purpose potting compost is also suitable but weighs rather more. A compost designed for hanging baskets is likely to contain water-retaining gel and a slow-release fertiliser.

Peat substitutes, such as coir fibre, are now being introduced as the concern of environmentalists about the depletion of natural peat bogs increases.

A soil-based mixture (multi-purpose compost), containing all necessary nutrients and trace elements, is usually used in windowboxes that are intended to last for more than one season, such as those containing small shrubs and alpines.

Ericaceous compost is necessary for lime-hating plants, such as hydrangeas, heathers, conifers and azaleas. Generally, this is best mixed with peat and sharp sand in the proportions 3:2:1.

Some specialist composts will contain small granules of Perlite or vermiculite, or tiny polystyrene balls. These are included to improve drainage and have no nutritional value.

Looking After Your Flowers

Watering

This is one of the most critical areas with hanging baskets and windowboxes as, once the root ball of a plant has dried out, it will prove very difficult to revive.

Watering is best carried out in the cooler part of the day, usually the morning or evening. Generally, the plants need to be in shade when you water, as water magnifies the sun's rays and can cause scorching of leaves and petals. Try to avoid getting water on leaves or petals.

In damp weather in winter, watering once weekly is all that is required. Never water when the temperature is at freezing or below as the roots will freeze

and be permanently damaged. In spring, water every few days depending on how warm and dry it is. Check the soil condition by pushing a finger deep into the compost in the box or basket. Do not assume that because the surface is damp, the rest of the compost will be too. In summer you need to water daily, especially on hot days when you may need to water twice or even three times if your basket is in a sunny position.

Use a watering can if you have only one or two baskets. The use of a rose on the can will prevent plants from being damaged. Let the basket absorb as much as half the amount of water in the can. If you can water the baskets on the ground, so much the better. If the water runs straight through, the compost may have dried out around the root balls of the individual plants. If this happens, water again ten minutes later and again ten minutes after that to help the compost become more absorbent again.

If you have a number of containers and baskets, a hose with a lance is the easiest way to water. A lance is a rigid hose extension with an on-off switch, which enables you to reach into high baskets without spraying water everywhere. Many hoses have a twist end which works as an on-off switch too.

To make watering baskets easier, you can buy a rise and fall attachment to bring the basket down for watering. These are sold in garden centres.

Another product now widely available is water-retaining gel which is available in granule form. This is mixed with water and added to the compost when planting up.

Should you discover that a basket has dried out, soak the whole basket in a

deep bucket of water, holding it under until air bubbles stop rising. Do not feed the basket until the soil has been moist for a few days.

A hand-held sprayer will give plants a quick pick-me-up but is no substitute for watering with a watering can or hose.

Alpines should be watered carefully in between the plants as the crowns of these plants do not like to be wet. You must use a watering can without a rose.

Herbs need less water than many other plants – not surprising when one considers their Mediterranean origins. Twice weekly should be adequate unless the weather is especially hot.

Feeding

There are two basic methods of feeding. You can use a slow-release fertiliser which is mixed in with the compost when planting, or a liquid or powder feed which is mixed in when watering.

If you choose to add feed when watering, you know exactly when the fertiliser is being applied. If you normally water by hose, you may wish to buy a special hose feed attachment which releases a small amount of fertiliser each time you press a trigger. Alternatively, you could revert to using a watering can for occasional feeding when watering.

Most nurseries and garden centres now include slow-release fertiliser granules when planting up baskets. Hanging basket compost often comes with fertiliser already mixed in so you will not need to fertilise again for a few weeks after planting.

If you choose to feed your baskets or boxes when watering, this should generally be done once a week. If you decide on a certain day of the week, you will be able to remember whether it has been done or not. Too much feed can damage plants but most manufacturers are aware of this and are fairly conservative about the amounts they recommend.

Pests and Problems

One of the nice things about hanging baskets and windowboxes is that, because they are off the ground, they don't tend to suffer so much from the common problem of slugs and snails which can inflict a great deal of damage. However, there are still insects and fungi which can cause problems and, should your plants look unhealthy, one of the first things to establish is what is wrong. The guide to symptoms given here should help.

Careful watering is particularly crucial on hot summer days as, once the roots are totally dry, they will not revive – you can only remove the plant and start again.

This is sometimes the easiest solution with diseased plants. The speedy removal of one plant can prevent the further spread of an infection, although sprays are often quickly effective. There is now a move towards the use of organic or rather simple soap sprays which do not involve using unnecessarily strong chemicals, although you may occasionally need to use a particular insecticide as specified.

Speedy treatment

Most of us are reluctant to spray but there are times when a serious disease or pest attack threatens. Aphids and caterpillars can cause severe damage. If this happens, select the right product – ask for advice at your garden centre and read the instructions carefully. Do not make the solution stronger than recommended and never use a spray can which has previously contained weedkiller. Choose a time when the weather is calm and cloudy, preferably the evening. Use a fine spray and spray until it is dripping from the leaves. Wash out the equipment and also wash your hands and face after spraying. Store the packet in a safe place, well-labelled and out of the reach of children and pets.

Plants that have been sprayed will benefit from a foliar feed, i.e. a liquid feed solution that is sprayed on to the leaves rather than put in the compost. This is one way to speed their recovery and promote healthy growth.

▼ **Leaf miner:** *white winding tunnels on marigold and chrysanthemum leaves which eventually turn brown. Treatment: destroy affected leaves. Spray the plant with fungicide.*

◀ **Rust:** *raised red, orange or brown spots. Commonly seen on pelargoniums, snapdragons, sweet william and chrysanthemums. Treatment: remove affected leaves. Spray with suitable fungicide.*

◀ **Wilt:** *can be due to lack of water or, if the plant is a snapdragon, chrysanthemum or poppy, it is likely to be a fungus. Treatment: remove plants and do not replant with the same species.*

▶ **Cold damage:** *frosts will cause leaves to curl and wilt – when they open the leaf will be yellow or even white. Treatment: remove affected leaves. Cover plants with protective fleece during cold nights.*

▶ **Powdery mildew:** *white surface to leaves caused by overcrowding and insufficient water. A disease seen on verbena, nigella and chrysanthemums. Treatment: spray with fungicide weekly.*

Pests: Symptoms and Cures

SIGNS TO LOOK FOR	PROBLEM	SOLUTION
Yellowing leaves	Overwatering	Water only once a week in winter, adjust according to shade in summer
Browning leaves	Underwatering	Water up to 3 times a day in hot spots and dry spells
Brown areas between leaf veins	Eelworm on phlox, asters, larkspur, calceolaria, chrysanthemum, zinnia and begonia	Pick off affected leaves
Wilt	If soil is moist could be a soil fungus on antirrhinum, aster, sweet pea or poppy	Remove plant; change compost
Grey mould (*Botrytis*) spots first, rotting occurs later	Humid weather	Pick off mouldy flowers and leaves. Spray with fungicide
Ragged petals	Whitefly or aphids on petunia, clarkia, zinnia; earwigs	Shake blooms; spray and place an inverted flower pot nearby
Distorted buds	Greenfly, blackfly (aphids); warm, dry weather	Use one of the many available sprays early on (organic or chemical)
Large holes in leaves	Caterpillars, woodlice, slugs and snails	Use a persistent insecticide; slug pellets
White tracks on the leaves (leaf miner)	Moth and fly larvae on columbines and chrysanthemums	Treat with a chemical spray
Powdery mildew	Fungi growing on begonias, chrysanthemums	Spray from early spring
Rust spots	Fungus on snapdragons, sweet williams, pelargoniums	Spray plants from early spring or destroy

Plant Lists

This listing gives details of the most commonly grown plants used for hanging baskets and windowboxes.

Alyssum, sweet (*Alyssum*)
- clumps of tiny flowers in white, pink, red and purple
- flowers late spring and summer
- well-drained potting compost
- full sun
- deadhead regularly
- very easy to grow

Artemisia absinthium
- attractive silver-grey foliage
- tiny yellow flowers spring to late summer
- leaves look best during summer months
- moist, well-drained potting compost
- full sun for foliage colour

Aster (*Aster*)
- daisy-like hardy perennials, mainly purples and pinks
- daisy-like autumn flowers
- rich well-drained potting mixture
- sun or semi-shade
- choose low-growing varieties

Begonia (*Begonia semperflorens*)
- vibrant flowers in pink, red, yellow or white
- summer-flowering with attractive green or brown leaves
- humus-rich (acid) potting mixture

- partial shade or shady site
- keep well watered, avoid splashing leaves
- can be kept over winter away from frosts
- feed weekly

Bergenia (elephant's ears) (*Bergenia*)
- large, shiny leathery leaves; tiny pink flower clusters
- hardy evergreen perennial with late summer, autumn and winter flowers
- poor, well-drained potting mixture
- sun or shade

Bidens aurea
- yellow, daisy-like flowers on wiry stems
- bushy trailing habit particularly suits hanging baskets
- plant in spring, flowers all summer
- well-drained potting compost
- prefers full sun but do not allow to dry out
- increasingly popular

Brachycome (*Brachycome*)
- small, daisy-like purple flowers
- summer-flowering
- good for hanging baskets
- well-drained potting compost
- prefers sunny site

Bugle (*Ajuga reptans*)
- attractive foliage plant; dark green/purple leaves
- tiny blue flowers on 20-cm (8 in) spikes from mid-spring to early summer
- rich, moist potting compost
- full sun to light shade
- hardy

Busy lizzie (*Impatiens*)
- prolific flowers in white, pink, red, lilac, orange
- flowers all summer long
- moist, well-drained potting mixture
- sun or shade
- keep watered in dry spells

Box (*Buxus sempervirens*)
- hardy evergreen shrub
- tiny leaves, compact growth
- well-drained soil
- sun or shade
- can be clipped into shapes

Cabbage, ornamental (*Brassica*)
- attractive autumn/winter foliage; pink, white and dark red varieties
- plant in autumn to last until spring
- prefers acidic potting mixture
- sunny site

Cacti (*Cacti*)
- succulent foliage plant, often with spikes or hairs
- flowers in summer, in winter also indoors
- free-draining compost
- sunny spot preferable
- hardy, can withstand drying out

Calceolaria (*Calceolaria*)
- bold flowers in purple, pink and white
- flowers all summer long
- moist but well-drained compost
- sun or shade
- keep well watered

Campanula (bellflower, Canterbury bell) (*Campanula*)
- delicate, blue, bell-shaped flowers

- flowers early to late summer
- moist but well-drained soil
- sun or shade
- trailing varieties have a long flowering period

Celosia (*Celosia*)
- brightly coloured 'feather duster' plumes
- summer-flowering
- well-drained compost
- sunny spot away from wind
- flowers are red, orange, yellow and pink

Chives (*Allium schoenoprasum*)
- herb with green fronds and pink flowers
- plant in spring for summer growth
- multi-purpose potting mixture
- full sun
- remove flowers to encourage foliage

Chrysanthemum (*Chrysanthemum*)
- large, daisy-like flowerheads, mainly orange, yellow and white
- late-summer- and autumn-flowering
- lightly limed soil is best
- sunny spot
- deadhead regularly
- spray against greenfly

Cineraria (senecio or dusty miller) (*Senecio*)
- large, silver-grey, intricate leaf
- plant out in spring for a long summer show
- any well-drained compost
- needs full sun for silvery leaves
- survives most mild winters
- remove small yellow flowers

Clary (*Salvia*)
- purple, pink and lilac spires of flowers
- summer-flowering
- chalky (alkaline) compost
- sunny site
- do not allow to dry out

Coleus (*Coleus blumei*)
- large, colourful leaves in brown, lime, orange, red, green and yellow combined
- plant out from late spring; survives to first frost
- well-drained mixture
- sun or semi-shade
- remove tiny blue flowers for bushy plant and leaf colour

Columbine (*Aquilegia*)
- tall, graceful flowers in lilac and pink
- spring and summer flowers
- dryish potting mixture
- sun or semi-shade
- hardy perennial; withstands wind and cold

Convolvulus (*Convolvulus*)
- trumpets of purple, pink and white flowers
- mid- to late-summer-flowering
- well-drained compost – not too rich
- full sun
- flowers open in the morning and die in the evening
- deadhead regularly

Cordyline (palm) (*Cordyline*)
- half-hardy/hardy shrub with lance-shaped leaves
- evergreen – withstands mild winters
- rich, well-drained potting compost
- sunny or semi-shady site
- a striking focal point to any display

Cornflower (*Centaurea*)
- blue, purple, pink and white flowers; green leaves have white underside
- early- to mid-summer-flowering
- well-drained potting compost; add lime if it is acidic
- full sun to light shade
- hardy

Cotoneaster (*Cotoneaster*)
- hardy shrub with glossy green leaves; red berries in autumn and winter
- evergreen
- well-drained compost
- sunny or semi-shady site
- withstands wind

Cowslip (*Primula veris*)
- pale yellow, scented flower
- large green leaves
- hardy, spring-flowering
- prefers chalky (alkaline) soil
- sun to semi-shade
- *never* lift from wild

Cranesbill, see Geranium

Creeping jenny (*Lysimachia nummularia*)
- attractive, light green trailing foliage
- yellow flowers, early to mid-summer
- prefers moist, rich compost
- sun or shade
- foliage will survive a mild winter

Crocus (*Crocus*)
- small, flowering bulbs (corms), mainly yellow, purple and white
- spring, autumn and winter flowers
- well-drained potting mixture
- prefers a sunny site
- withstands cold well

Curry plant (*Helichrysum augustifolium*)
- silver grey foliage with white or pink flowers
- fairly hardy evergreen shrub, summer flowers
- ericaceous (acidic) soil
- sunny site
- protect from frosts

Cyclamen (*Cyclamen*)
- delicate flowers on stems, in red, white or pink
- winter-flowering perennial
- very rich, well-drained potting mixture
- sunny or semi-shady site
- will not withstand temperatures below freezing
- suitable for sheltered town sites
- grown from corms – do not water top of plant

Cypress (*Chamaecyparis*)
- needle-like foliage in shades from dark green to yellow
- evergreen – year-round foliage
- well-drained, acid potting mixture
- sun or shade
- choose dwarf or low-growing varieties
- leave in pot to restrict growth
- keep watered in dry spells

Daffodil (*Narcissus*)
- trumpet flowers in shades of yellow
- spring-flowering bulbs, plant in autumn or buy pot-grown in early spring
- light or well-drained compost
- sun or light shade
- miniature varieties available
- hardy

Dahlias (*Dahlia*)
- bushy perennial grown from tuber; large flowerheads with 8 petals
- summer- and autumn-flowering
- well-drained potting mixture
- sunny site
- feed and water regularly

Daisy (African, Swan River, Cape marigold) (*Bellis perennis, Dimorphotheca barberiae*)
- hardy flowering plants in pinks, yellow and white
- spring- and summer-flowering; varieties differ
- rich, well-drained potting mixture
- sunny or semi-shady site
- deadhead regularly for repeat flowering
- some trailing, i.e. Swan River

Deadnettle (*Lamium maculatum*)
- attractive green and white variegated foliage
- pink or purple flowers mid- to late summer
- moist, rich potting compost
- prefers medium to light shade
- feed in spring
- remove dead flowers

Diascia (*Diascia*)
- arching sprays of dark pink to mid-purple flowers, 30 cm (12 in) long, hardy
- prolific flowers mid- to late summer
- well-drained potting compost
- full sun to light shade
- plant spring to early autumn

Eucalyptus (blue gum)
(*Eucalyptus*)
- attractive, lance-shaped leaf
- foliage is at its peak through summer and early autumn
- multi-purpose potting compost
- sun or semi-shade
- grown for its blue green foliage

Euonymus (*Euonymus*)
- tough, variegated foliage plant
- choose hardy, evergreen varieties
- well-drained potting compost
- sun or semi-shade
- attractive leaf colours; very hardy

Felicia (kingfisher daisy, blue marguerite) (*Felicia bergeriana*)
- yellow-centred, blue, daisy-like plants on fine wiry stems
- summer-flowering
- well-drained compost
- full sun, can withstand wind
- trailing habit makes it effective in baskets
- petals close in dull weather

Fennel (*Foeniculum vulgare*)
- herb with feathery green foliage, small yellow flowers; leaves used for flavouring food
- flowers and foliage early to late summer
- light, i.e. not rich, well-drained potting compost
- full sun to very light shade
- can grow to 60 cm (2 ft) in height

Ferns, see nephrolepis and maidenhair

Feverfew (*Chrysanthemum parthenium*)
- hardy herb with small, white, daisy-like flowers and feathery leaf
- flowers early summer to early autumn
- any compost
- full sun to light shade
- can be used for medicinal purposes

Flossflower (*Ageratum*)
- strong blue-mauve feathery flowers
- flowers mid-summer to early autumn
- sun or some shade
- standard potting compost
- deadhead regularly for flowers

Forget-me-not (*Myosotis*)
- tiny spring flowers in blue, pink and white
- flowers early spring to early summer
- rich, well-drained potting mixture
- full sun to light shade

Fuchsia (*Fuchsia*)
- cascading blooms in shades of pink and red; trailing and upright varieties
- stunning summer and autumn flowers
- moist, well-drained compost
- sheltered shady or semi-shady site
- particularly suitable for baskets and boxes
- liquid feed weekly
- can be damaged by heavy rain

Gaultheria (*Gaultheria*)
- attractive shrub with red berries and small, glossy leaves
- evergreen; berries in autumn and winter
- damp acidic (ericaceous) potting mixture
- grows well in shade or semi-shade

Gazania (*Gazania*)
- daisy-like flowers that open in the sun
- summer-flowering
- sandy, free-draining compost
- sunny site

Geranium (dusky cranesbill) (*Geranium*)
- small pink flowers on dark green stems
- early-summer- to early-autumn-flowering
- tolerant of soil conditions as long as compost is not waterlogged
- full sun to light shade
- prolific flowers all summer long

Grape hyacinth (*Muscari*)
- spikes of small purple blue flowers
- spring-flowering bulbs
- well-drained potting mixture
- sun or shade
- delicately scented flowers

Gypsophila (*Gypsophila*)
- masses of tiny white flowers
- spring and summer flowers
- well-drained potting compost
- sunny situation
- these dry well

Heathers (*Erica/Calluna*)
- hardy, evergreen shrub that has pink and white varieties
- plant in mid-autumn for year-round foliage; varieties flower each month of the year
- well-drained acidic (ericaceous) compost
- sunny site
- useful winter-flowering plant

Hebe (*Hebe*)
- spiky foliage; short plumes of purple flowers
- hardy evergreen shrub; flowers late summer and autumn
- prefers well-drained potting compost
- sunny site
- protect from frost
- can grow up to 60 cm (2 ft) tall

Helianthemum (rock rose) (*Helianthemum*)
- alpines with delicate flowerheads on fine wiry stems; soft grey green foliage
- spring- and summer-flowering
- well-drained, half-gritted potting compost
- sunny situation

Helichrysum (*Helichrysum*)
- double, daisy-like flowers in orange, pink and white; also silvery grey foliage types, e.g. *Helichrysum petiolatum*
- summer and autumn flowers
- well-drained potting mixture
- sunny site important
- flowers dry well for arranging

Heliotrope (*Heliotropium*)
- scented purple flowers in clusters
- summer-flowering
- rich, well-drained potting compost
- sunny site
- do not allow to dry out
- delicately scented

Hellebore (Christmas rose) (*Helleborus*)
- white flowers, dark green foliage
- winter and early spring flowers
- well-drained, moist potting compost
- semi-shady situation

Holly (*Ilex*)
- attractive shiny foliage with spikes
- hardy evergreen; red berries in winter
- well-drained potting mixture
- sun or shade
- trailing and climbing varieties available

Hosta (*Hosta*)
- large attractive leaves, some variegated
- one or two tall flower spires in summer
- moist, well-drained soil
- sun or shade
- some varieties are scented

Houseleek (*Sempervivum*)
- rosette of succulent pointed leaves
- summer flowers; use in alpine box
- shallow, well-drained potting compost containing grit
- sunny position

Hyacinth (*Hyacinthus*)
- thick spikes of scented flowers; pink, blue and white most popular
- spring-flowering bulbs
- well-drained potting compost
- sunny or semi-shady site
- dwarf varieties available

Hydrangea (*Hydrangea*)
- a hardy shrub with full flowerheads
- large summer flowerheads dry well
- prefers rich, moist, but well-drained, potting compost
- sun or semi-shade
- prefers ericaceous soil

Iris, dwarf (*Iris reticulata*)
- striking blue flower on strong stem
- plant autumn bulbs for late-winter, early-spring flowers
- keep compost moist through winter
- sunny situation, can withstand cold
- dwarf varieties suit windowboxes

Ivy (*Hedera helix*)
- useful foliage plant with attractive leaf shape, some variegated
- hardy evergreen, can be used year round
- moist soil conditions
- shade-loving
- trailing varieties can be used to cover basket chains and handles

Juniper (spreading fir) (*Juniperus*)
- needle-like foliage, low-growing
- evergreen; bright berries midwinter
- prefers acid soil
- sunny site if possible

Lady's mantle (*Alchemilla mollis*)
- tiny powdery-yellow flowers; attractive yellow green foliage
- flowers all summer
- well-drained compost
- sunny situation
- particularly suits windowboxes and baskets

Laurel, spotted (*Aucuba japonica*)
- attractive, large, spotted, mid-green leaves
- evergreen
- standard potting compost
- sun or shade
- easy to grow

Lavender (*Lavandula*)
- scented grey green leaves; some varieties silvery
- purple flowers in summer
- rich, well-drained compost
- prefers a sunny site

Lemon balm (*Melissa officinalis*)
- attractive, scented foliage
- white flowers mid-summer
- light, well-drained compost
- full sun
- remove flowers for increased foliage

Leucothoe (*Leucothoe*)
- attractive foliage plant; leaves turn red in autumn
- evergreen shrub, good for autumn/winter colour; white flowers in spring and early summer
- moist, acidic (ericaceous) potting mixture
- shade or semi-shade

Lily, African (*Agapanthus*)
- blue or white, delicate, bell-shaped flowers
- summer-flowering
- moist potting mixture, well drained
- sunny situation
- deadhead regularly

Lily of the valley (*Convallaria*)
- delicate white, winter blooms
- fragrant, early-spring flowers

- moist potting mixture
- sun or semi-shade
- grow from rhizomes

Lobelia (*Lobelia*)
- popular, bushy, trailing plant in blues, purple and, recently, dark red varieties
- flowers for one season only, from early to late summer
- moist, well-drained mixture
- sun or semi-shade
- do not allow to dry out

Maidenhair fern (*Adiantum*)
- fern with delicate, attractive foliage
- year-round foliage in moist conditions
- damp, neutral to acid potting mixture
- shady or semi-shady site
- do not allow to dry out

Maple, Japanese (*Acer palmatum*)
- hardy shrub with unusual dark leaves
- deciduous
- rich, well-drained potting compost
- sun or semi-shade
- container restricts growth, so it is suitable for boxes

Marguerite, golden (chamomile) (*Anthemis*)
- daisy-like flowers in white and yellow
- summer-flowering
- parsley-like foliage
- well-drained potting compost
- sunny position
- deadhead regularly

Marigold pot; French (*Calendula; Tagetes*)
- orange, cream and yellow flowers in various sizes
- spring, summer and autumn flowers

107

- any well-drained potting compost
- sunny situation preferred
- deadhead regularly

Mint (*Mentha*)
- strong-smelling herb; leaves used for mint sauce
- best from late spring to late summer
- any potting compost but not too dry
- full sun to very light shade
- can be invasive, keep in pot

Monkey flower (*Mimulus*)
- pretty, bell-like flowers with spotted 'monkey' face in yellow, orange and red
- summer-flowering
- moist compost
- prefers sunny situation
- deadhead regularly

Nasturtiums (*Tropaeolum*)
- orange, red and yellow annuals and perennials
- edible flowers in late summer
- well-drained potting compost
- sunny site

Nemesia (*Nemesia*)
- prolific small flowers in a wide variety of colours
- summer-flowering, short-lived if dry
- lime-free potting compost
- sun or light shade
- keep well watered
- easy to grow from seed

Nepeta, see Swedish ivy

Nephrolepis fern (*Nephrolepis*)
- attractive, arching fronds of foliage
- year-round leaf interest
- rich, moist potting mixture
- light sun to deep shade

Nicotiana, see tobacco plant

Oxalis (*Oxalis adenophylla*)
- cloverlike leaf; small yellow flowers in clusters
- flowers late spring to early autumn
- full sun to light shade
- light, open, sandy soil
- water and feed frequently

Palm, see cordyline

Pansy (*Viola*)
- prolific easy-to-grow flowers in many shades
- summer- and winter-flowering varieties
- well-drained, moist compost
- any situation, sun or shade
- deadhead regularly

Parsley (*Petroselinum*)
- herb with attractive, fine foliage, used for cooking and decoration
- plant late spring for summer growth; dies with frost
- moist, well-drained soil
- sunny site
- trim regularly to encourage growth

Pelargonium (*Pelargonium*)
- easy-to-grow bold flowers, some with scented leaves, many varieties available
- plant out after frosts for summer-flowering; can be year-round if kept in a warm and sunny spot in winter, i.e. greenhouse or windowsill inside
- dryish, well-drained potting mixture
- more flowers in a sunny site
- take cuttings in late summer for propagation

Penstemon, beard tongue (*Penstemon*)

- delicate, foxglove-like blooms in pinks, reds and purples
- early- to late-summer-flowering
- rich, well-drained potting compost
- prefers light shade; tolerates full sun

Periwinkle (*Vinca*)
- evergreen shrub with glossy leaves
- purple flowers in spring
- well-drained potting mixture
- sun or shade
- attractive trailing foliage

Petunias, multiflora, floribunda, grandiflora (*Petunia*)
- prolific flower trumpets in striking red, purple, pink and white with striped and starred hybrids
- non-stop summer to autumn flowers
- well-drained potting mixture
- sun or semi-shade
- look out for new trailing hybrid – 'Surfinia'
- some lightly scented

Phlox (*Phlox*)
- tightly massed flowerheads in white, yellow, pink and purple
- flowers late spring to late summer
- any well-drained potting compost
- sunny site
- choose dwarf varieties

Pick-a-back plant (*Tolmiea*)
- attractive, pale green foliage, with small leaves growing just above larger ones
- can survive year round if

climate is not severe
- well-drained, slightly acid potting compost
- shade or semi-shade
- plantlets can be propagated

Pinks (*Dianthus*)
- tufted flowers in pink and white; scented and variegated varieties available
- hardy evergreen foliage; summer flowers
- well-drained potting compost
- sunny site
- deadhead regularly

Plectranthus (*Plectranthus*)
- attractive trailing foliage
- tender perennials, some evergreen
- moist potting compost
- sun or semi-shade
- cut back straggly growth

Polyanthus (*Primula*)
- cross between cowslip and primrose with masses of bright blooms in clusters on stalks; many shades available
- early-spring-flowering
- any moist potting compost
- semi-shade preferable

Poppy (*Papaver*)
- delicate blooms on fine stems; yellows, reds and pinks
- colourful summer flowers
- light, well-drained soil
- sun or semi-shade
- alpine varieties do well

Portulaca (sun plant) (*Portulaca*)
- succulent, fleshy-leaved plants with brightly coloured flowers
- summer-flowering
- well-drained sandy soil
- needs full sun

Primrose (*Primula*)
- popular spring plant with

long, wide leaves and bright, rewarding flowers
- plant in late winter/early spring for flowers early to mid-spring
- moist, rich potting compost
- light to medium shade
- yellow varieties are scented

Ranunculus (Persian buttercup) (*Ranunculus asiaticus*)
- brightly coloured peony-like flower with masses of petals in yellow, deep and pale pink, white with pink edging
- late-spring flowers
- moist, but well-drained, potting mixture
- full sun to semi-shade
- grown from tubers

Rock rose, see helianthemum

Rosa (*Rosa*)
- attractive clusters of flower petals, thorny stems; some fragrant
- flowers spring and summer
- moist, well-drained compost
- sunny site
- choose miniature varieties for containers

Rudbeckia (*Rudbeckia*)
- large, daisy-like flowers in red, orange and yellow
- late-summer-, early-autumn-flowering
- well-drained potting compost
- sun or light shade
- choose dwarf varieties

Sage (*Salvia*)
- hardy evergreen herb with soft grey green foliage
- summer and autumn flowers

- well-drained potting mixture
- sunny site
- some have aromatic or variegated foliage

Santolina (*Santolina*)
- hardy evergreen shrub with scented silver foliage
- yellow summer flowers
- well-drained potting mixture
- sunny site
- good for year-round interest

Saponaria, see tumbling ted

Scabious (*Scabiosa*)
- hardy plant with pincushion-like, pale, cornflower-blue flowers
- late-summer-flowering
- rich, well-drained potting mixture (not acidic)
- sunny site
- some scented varieties

Scilla (*Scilla*)
- spikes of small blue flowers
- spring-flowering bulbs
- well-drained potting compost
- sun or semi-shade

Sedum (*Sedum*)
- attractive, fleshy or succulent foliage
- summer to autumn flowers
- well-drained potting mixture
- sunny site
- do not overwater

Senecio (*Senecio*)
- attractive silver leaves
- daisy-like flowers in spring, summer and autumn
- well-drained potting mixture
- sun or semi-shade

Silene (*Silene*)
- annuals and perennials

- flowers in late spring to the end of summer
- well-drained, gritted compost
- sun or semi-shade
- do not allow to become waterlogged

Sisyrinchium (*Sisyrinchium*)
- yellow flowers on upright spikes
- flowers mid- to late summer
- light, well-drained, humus-rich compost
- full sun
- grows to 60 cm (2 ft) tall

Skimmia (*Skimmia*)
- evergreen shrub; red berries in autumn
- sweet-scented white/pink flowers in spring
- moisture-retaining potting compost
- sun or shade

Snapdragon (*Antirrhinum*)
- flower trumpets in red, yellow, orange and brown
- spring to autumn flowers
- rich, well-drained potting compost
- flowers open in sun
- deadhead regularly
- choose dwarf varieties where possible

Snowberries (*Symphoricarpos*)
- white, globular fruit; evergreen foliage
- spring flowers; winter fruit
- moist potting compost
- semi-shade
- fruits are poisonous

Snow-in-summer (*Cerastium tomentosum*)
- hardy, flowering plant with pretty silver foliage
- prolific white flowers late

spring to early summer
- any potting compost
- full sun
- trim regularly

Sorrel (*Rumex*)
- red-green herb with upright, feathery foliage
- plant in spring for summer use
- well-drained potting compost
- full sun

Spurge (*Euphorbia*)
- foliage plants with attractive fleshy leaves
- spring flowers
- moist, but well-drained, compost
- sun or semi-shade
- can irritate skin

Stocks (*Matthida*)
- multiple, scented blooms on spires; many shades available
- flowering mid-spring and mid-summer
- well-drained potting compost, not acidic
- sun or light shade
- lingering fragrance

Strawberry, wild (*Fragaria*)
- hardy plant with attractive trailing foliage, white or pink flowers and edible summer fruit
- plant mid-autumn to mid-spring for flowers in late spring and fruit throughout summer months
- well-drained potting compost
- sunny site
- cut away unwanted runners

Sunflower (*Helianthus*)
- bright, giant, daisy-like flowers in yellow, red and orange, with brown centres

- mid-summer-flowering
- any potting compost
- full sun
- compact varieties available

Surfinia, see petunia

Swedish ivy (*Nepeta hederacea variegata*)
- attractive green and white trailing foliage
- perennial
- well-drained potting compost
- full sun or light shade

Sweet william (*Dianthus barbatus*)
- flattened heads of sweet-smelling pink flowers
- flowers in late spring and summer
- well-drained potting compost, not acidic
- sunny situation
- dwarf varieties available

Tarragon, French (*Artemisia dranunculus*)
- spiky upright herb; aromatic grey green foliage
- plant in spring for summer-long use
- well-drained potting compost
- sunny situation
- trim to promote growth

Thrift (*Armeria maritima*)
- evergreen alpine
- deep pink flowers in early to late summer
- well-drained potting compost
- full sun
- does not like wet winters

Thuja (*Thuja*)
- conifer with needle-like foliage in shades of green, grey and yellow
- acidic soil
- any situation

- do not allow to dry out

Thyme (*Thymus*)
- hardy evergreen herb with attractive, scented leaves
- white flowers in summer
- moist, well-drained potting mixture
- sunny site
- remove flowers for foliage growth

Tobacco plant (*Nicotiana*)
- fairly hardy, tall foliage with prolific flowers
- long-lasting summer flowers
- rich, well-drained potting compost
- likes semi-shade or shade
- some varieties scented
- can grow to 60 cm (2 ft)

Tomato, tumbler
- trailing plants with cherry-size tomatoes
- shoots do not need pinching out
- small yellow flowers in early summer, fruits mid- to late summer
- rich, moist compost
- sunny site
- keep well fed and watered

Tradescantia (*Tradescantia*)
- very hardy, trailing foliage, some pink-edged
- house plants that do well outside in summer
- well-drained potting mixture – not fussy
- sun or semi-shade
- bring in before first frosts

Tulip (*Tulipa*)
- hardy perennial grown from bulb
- colourful spring flowers
- well-drained alkaline potting mixture
- sun or semi-shade
- choose dwarf varieties

Tumbling ted (*Saponaria ocymoides*)
- profuse, rose-pink flowers
- flowers in mid-summer to early autumn
- thrives on well-drained compost
- sunny site
- compact, prostrate, tumbling growth

Verbena (*Verbena*)
- colourful trailing clusters of summer flowers, mostly pinks and purples, good for baskets
- summer-flowering
- well-drained potting mixture
- sun or semi-shade
- some scented varieties

Veronica (*Veronica*)
- attractive spires of blue or pink flowers
- mid- to late-summer-flowering
- any potting compost
- full sun to light shade
- miniature and alpine varieties available

Violet, sweet (*Viola odorata*)
- small-headed, fragrant pansy
- different varieties flower all year round
- well-drained potting mixture
- any site, sun or shade
- deadhead regularly

Wallflower (*Cheiranthus cheiri*)
- colourful massed petals on upright stems; red and yellow most commonly seen
- spring-flowering
- well-drained alkaline potting compost – adding garden lime (chalk) will help
- sunny spot
- choose shorter varieties

INDEX

ACKNOWLEDGEMENTS

The author would like to thank the following people for their help on
Windowboxes and Hanging Baskets:

Frankie Annis, Graham Wallis, Mr J. Wilson and Mr S. Curtis for horticultural help and advice. Also Mr and Mrs M. Fordham, Mr and Mrs J. Mustoe, Miss R. Amy, Mr and Mrs B. Barham, Mrs L. Allen and Mr P. Hiscocks, Mr and Mrs R. McLellan, Mr and Mrs R. Osborn, Mr and Mrs I. Fletcher, Mr and Mrs A. Knight, Mr and Mrs A. Tilbury, Mr and Mrs J. Wilson, Mr and Mrs Woore, Mrs J. Harper, Mr and Mrs Melville, Mr and Mrs C. Arnold, Mr P. Garnier, Mr and Mrs Huxley, Mrs H. Yeomans, Mrs J. Lewis, Mrs L. Fairholm, Mrs S. Ravenhill, Mrs W. Ellard, Dr E. Biggs, Mr and Mrs Mendelsohn, Saffron Walden nursery school and all the residents of Hampton, Middlesex for kindly allowing us to photograph in their gardens.

Project editor Gill MacLennan for all her assistance with planting and photography, gardening editor Lesley Young and Maggie Aldred who art directed with care and precision. Also John Clarke at Garson Farm Garden Centre in Esher and Liz Gage, Caroline Owen, Sally Spicer and Dot and Caroline of Scotsdale Garden Centre, Great Shelford, Cambridge, for the supply of plants, containers and advice.

Special thanks to photographers Spike Powell and Glyn Barney for their enthusiasm and commitment.

Chelsea Flower Show Exhibitors: Hermitage Horticultural Society,
The Allotment Holders Association, The Harrow Show, Shipdham Horticultural Society, The Royal Hospital, Berkshire College of Agriculture, Brightling Flower Show Society, Horton Cum Studley Horticultural Society, Kingston Horticultural Society.

Specialist Suppliers
Containers
Webbs, Unit 2, 15 Station Road, Knebworth, Stevenage, Herts SG3 6AP
Scotsdale Garden Centre, Cambridge Road, Great Shelford, Cambridge CB2 5JT
The Terracotta Shop, 8 Moorfield Road, Duxford, Cambridgeshire

Plants
F. Annis, 51 North Road, Abington, Cambridgeshire
Grace's Farm Shop, nr Thaxted, Essex
Ickleton Trout Farm & Nursery, Frogge Street, Ickleton, Cambridgeshire
Springwell Nurseries, Josephs Farm, Springwell, Little Chesterford, Essex
Siskin Plants (alpines) Woodbridge, Suffolk
Squires Garden Centre, Sixth Cross Road, Twickenham, Middlesex
Putney Garden Centre, Upper Richmond Road, Putney SW15
Garson Farm Garden Centre, Winterdown Road, West End, Esher, Surrey

Also for loan of faux lead windowbox
Capital Garden Products, Gibbs Reed Barn, Pashley Road, Ticehurst,
East Sussex TN5 7HE